Given in Memory
Of
Howard Dunbar

May 22, 1995

BOOKS BY JOHN HAY

A Private History *(Poems)*

The Run

Nature's Year

A Sense of Nature *(with Arlene Strong)*

The Great Beach

The Atlantic Shore *(with Peter Farb)*

In Defense of Nature

The Primal Alliance: Earth and Ocean

Spirit of Survival

The Undiscovered Country

The Immortal Wilderness

The Bird of Light

The Bird of Light

by JOHN HAY

W · W · NORTON & COMPANY

New York · London

Copyright © 1991 by John Hay
All rights reserved.

Printed in the United States of America.

The text of this book is composed in Bulmer,
with the display set in University.
Composition by and Manufacturing by Maple Vail Book Manufacturing Group.
Book design by Antonina Krass.

Library of Congress Cataloging-in-Publication Data

Hay, John, 1915–
The bird of light / John Hay.
p.   cm.
1. Terns.   I. Title.
QL696.C46H388   1991
598′.338—dc20   90-21041

ISBN 0-393-02995-6
W.W. Norton & Company, Inc., 500 Fifth Avenue, New York, N.Y. 10110
W.W. Norton & Company, Ltd., 10 Coptic Street, London WC1A 1PU
2 3 4 5 6 7 8 9 0

To Helen Hays

CONTENTS

Contents 10

≈

FOREWORD

The Bird of Light follows a book I wrote about terns entitled *Spirit of Survival,* published by E. P. Dutton in 1974. Although I have incorporated some passages from the earlier book into the present text, *The Bird of Light* is an entirely new book.

I am especially indebted to Alan Poole, biologist, and author of *Ospreys,* who generously offered to read my manuscript. He was in every way helpful with his suggestions for improvement. I am also grateful to Jim Mairs of Norton for his patience.

I have talked with many people over the years who have had some knowledge of terns. My friend Helen Hays, Director of the Great Gull Island Program, plunged me into their midst at an early stage, and I learned a great deal from her. I have also consulted Dr. William S. Drury and Dr. Ian Nisbet on several occasions. Their professional knowledge and devotion to terns and other seabirds has been invaluable. And I should not forget all those students and tern wardens who monitor terns on the summer beaches every year. They are the kind of pioneers in conservation that the world is much in need of.

The Bird of Light

Migrants in Winter

Day one is any day in the year. Leaves are born this minute; winter or summer, flowers never die. The fish circle on within the greater circles of the sea, and the birds in their migrations translate affinities from one hemisphere to another. This is the law of coexistent life which carries with it vast expenditure and sacrifice and is all we ourselves depend on for continuance. It is that day in which I, neither optimistic nor pessimistic about human prospects, look out over land and sea for more enduring guides, those who have practiced earth's art for periods of time which may be calculated by the human mind but are really incalculable in their changes. This has led me to see what we put down as mere birds as carriers of light and wisdom.

I have now had a love affair with terns for many years, even though these tirelessly flying, excitable, vulnerable birds have seldom come very close to me, having more often spun out of sight. That they keep returning to their nesting territories on home shores has become a source of restoration for me. These ancient travelers tie all shores together. Like other migrants, they will always be at a distance from me, but that only keeps me reaching after them. It is the essence of love in our experience that it keeps us half in turmoil, rejecting and rejected, torn away, rejoined again. All things move ahead in accordance with a passion endowed with immortal principles, like the earth itself.

I will never wholly know the terns because of the facts and information I am able to collect about them. I follow after them because the quality of their being is still wild, still unconquerable, out of the ocean of being that created them.

A few miles from where I live on Cape Cod, there is a raised island, or dune promontory, locally called Gray's Beach, where a colony of common and roseate terns have been nesting for many years. It lies out on the far rim of an extensive salt marsh, and is made up of sandy hummocks and hollows, shelving off into saltwater from a narrow beach that merges with eroding banks of peat and a scanty growth of spartina grass. It is not literally an island except during periods of storm tides, when it is surrounded, and at times invaded, by water, but for the terns it is an island of nurture between their arrival in May and their departure in August.

Now, in early winter, the salt marsh and Gray's Beach are bare and silent but for the wind and the distant roaring of the surf off outer bars. The dead stalks of the beach grass that keep the low dunes from blowing and breaking out are straw yellow, with a ragged look at the butt like old cornstalks. When I last walked out there in September, many terns were beating back and forth over offshore waters, diving for fish, but they had left their nesting areas behind them. It was then that I picked up the light and delicate skull of a tern with very large eye cavities and dully polished like a white pebble, with a faintly oily sheen. That suggested nightly visits from a great-horned owl. Repeated and consistent raids by that formidable predator, which will tear an adult tern's head off, can result in the complete desertion of a colony. At the very least, since the owl keeps the terns off their nests, night after night, a large number of eggs will fail to hatch out and chicks will die.

I also found a fragile cup, all that was left of a broken egg shell, a symbol of where life begins, the shell of the womb, the shape of the globe itself. Gray's Beach is close enough to mainland predators so as not to provide the best conditions for the terns, who prefer off-shore islands less exposed to owls and marauding mammals. The better sites have been lost to them, principally because of an over-whelming population of gulls, the result of the vast supply of waste food we have opened up to them in the twentieth century. Still, Gray's Beach once sheltered a tern colony of several thousand pairs, which kept up its number for some years before it started to decline.

Tidal marshes are sheltered by offshore sandbars and barrier beaches, and their growth takes advantage of the embayments along the shoreline. The winds blow freely across their open ranges, and their tough, salt-resistant grasses seem to hold the year in place. Natural channels and manmade ditches take the tidewaters through all levels of a marsh, rising up and flooding over, then falling and withdrawing, a daily, nightly, permanent rhythm to which all its life is responsive.

A great blue heron, that almost spectral image of a prehistoric past, rises majestically out of the marsh, on big, bowed, misty gray-blue wings, then settles down some distance further on, disappearing into the confines of a ditch. A winter that freezes over creeks, ponds, and marshes for too long a time may be deadly for a heron. It may starve to death, although in an environment tempered by the heat-retaining capacity of the ocean, it may survive.

During a mild winter, some shorebirds may linger through December. On land, robins, an occasional thrush, and a few song-birds may find enough to feed on throughout the winter. On rela-tively warm and sunny winter days, some insects will appear before you in the air. The subtleties, the fine points of contact, between these lives and the surrounding world largely escape us who merely claim it as our exclusive territory. What do I know of the earth that its prior inhabitants are not already aware of?

We have to wait until late April or early May for the terns to start coming in from such far distant shores as Trinidad, Surinam, and

Brazil, but life continually moves in coastal waters, and some inshore migration is still alive. Over the exposed flats at low tide, flocks of gray and white sanderlings, with many brown dunlins intermixed, are deftly probing the surface for tiny crustaceans or mollusks. I have seen flocks of a thousand or more in December and early January. A dog races in their direction, and a big flock instantaneously divides in two, each part skimming low, wheeling away, and settling down out of reach. At other times, they rise up, dip, turn, and swing like a casting of silver facets into the air, or dancing flowers, alternating the dark shading of their backs and the white of their bellies. When they flip over on their sides, reflecting the sunlight, it is as if they were deliberately courting it.

Such dazzling unanimity is as much a puzzle to those who try to unravel it as are the currents of a running brook. These birds are apparently without leadership, though they move as one, and at the same time the flock is made up of individuals who are acutely aware of their neighbors, and the spacing they need to fly with them. Their grace and precision derives from impulses over which human life has no control. Yet if this complex art eludes us, it is as spontaneous as the sight we receive it with. Is it not possible to follow the light through the medium of a bird? Without them, the days would go by without definition.

The sunrise, saffron and red, bleeds along the horizon above the trees, topped with small black clouds like a band of stylized waves. The day moves on, and a cold, brilliant northern light is cast over coastal waters winnowed and skewed around by the wind. As the morning sun begins to warm a thin coating of ice left by the high tide along the banks of the salt marsh, little white flakes suddenly snap off and fly up like so many flags. On the marsh level the grasses are matted down, like the coarse hairs of a dead deer I once came across in the dunes, while the cold wind whistles over them. A crow flies by, and then a Canada goose, a lone bugler looking for its companions.

Winter backs and fills with its polar opposites of light and dark. Periodic storms lock us in and inhibit most travel, but winter is a traveler in itself, moving on and out like the ocean waves that follow the future, on the forward edge of light. We hide from its reality, in the name, not entirely unjustified, of security. Winter is part death, part glory.

Arctic signs keep melting and reappearing, like the snow that gathers on the trees and in patches over the dunes. On a day between storms, sky and water work together over the open Atlantic on majestic variations in form. There are snowy caves in the dark cloud curtains over the sea, and low-lying cloud mountains ringing the horizon. Great dark wands reach into a gray sky where a few herring gulls are circling like hawks on fall migration over a mountain ridge. Bad weather, with high winds and sleet, is predicted after nightfall, but the tables of the sea are now flat and calm, and over them the waterfowl collaborate in waiting for the earth's next move. Hundreds of eider ducks raft off the cliffed shores; red-breasted mergansers cast over the surface like feathered lances; and Canada geese ride high on the waters like stately vessels. The great transformations of the winter sea and sky consign the world we ourselves construct to a makeshift status.

Throughout the month of December, people reported dead humpback whales floating offshore, and some were carried in by wind and tides. They died of causes so far undetermined, although it is thought that they may have been poisoned by mackerel which had ingested a toxic red algae. On December 13, the body of one of those playful, singing giants landed close to a nearby beach off Cape Cod Bay. The body was at first blown up out of all proportion by the gases of decay, since it must have been dead for some days. Then it collapsed after one side was cut away to make samples of flesh for analysis. It was the eleventh humpback to be reported, plus two minke whales.

Following a fierce storm, with temperatures well below freezing, light snow and a high wind that blew for twenty-four hours, the world was still dark along the shore. The black, grooved hide of the whale, which was thirty-seven feet long, sagged on its thick bed of rime ice. After struggling to reach it through the frozen mush, a few quiet onlookers stood around the body, paying their respects, and after a short time departed.

I measured the width of the flukes at twelve feet. A white flipper, a third of the whale's length, extended stiffly from its side, and the internal organs where the body had been cut away bore some resemblance to our own, enormously enlarged. They were a revelation of earth colors, in shades of red, gray, and a drab green, a dark interior now exposed to a dark day and an atmosphere of mourning. I sensed an unspoken question among us, common to the age, which has to do with how much injury our world is responsible for. We are continually faced with the vast disparity between man's power to destroy and his inability to control or foresee the consequences. What might be happening out there in deeper waters to further reduce the sum of life? If we leave the whales behind us, do we risk the loss of all we know within us of the ocean's power and stability?

Small flocks of dunlins and sanderlings are still active along the shore, running forward on twinkling legs, picking up their food out of the exposed sand and mud flats at low tide. Wild, fast-moving storms blow in with sleet and snow and then clear off and away, and the little birds keep reappearing. I find their tracks, like skeletons of leaves, etched in the wet sand of the beach. So long as their food supply is not covered over by ice, some will have enough to feed on.

Sanderlings have an extraordinary range. They are scattered across the planet, from North to South America, across the Atlantic to Britain, over the Mediterranean and Caspian seas to Burma, Indonesia, and Australia and, as the *Audubon Encyclopedia of Birds* ends the account, "etc.," a cosmopolitan, nearly universal migrant. They are very hardy little birds, pearly everlastings, like the flowers of that name. Dead shorebirds are seldom found; they get lost to wind and wave. They are like flecks of foam, ephemeral, though in that life and death context, omnipotent. Yet in recent years, the sanderling population has plummeted for reasons that are not entirely clear.

A few days and nights of below-freezing January weather, and ice begins to pack up along the shore until its broken white masses extend far out over the saltwaters of the bay, brilliant in the sunlight.

The sanderlings, with their food supply covered up, have disappeared from the local beaches. Since 400 miles a day is no problem for them, they might have flown to better feeding grounds far to the south of us, or found an ice-free shore on some other part of the Cape. It only takes a few days of sun and moderating temperatures to disperse the ice far and wide over the horizon, and a few small flocks reappear to feed over the now exposed flats. Sea ducks also move into the reopened waters. A great black-back gull picks away at the floating body of a young eider, shot by a random gunner, and has a hard time getting through its dense coat of down and feathers. Many gulls find food in lines of seaweed dislodged from offshore beds by ice and storm waves, to be washed in by the tides. Crab legs and bits of their shells litter the beach. Gulls are always waiting to seize their opportunities.

The little gray and white sanderlings keep reappearing at mid to low tide. If mud and sand are so frozen that the invertebrates they feed on are no longer accessible, these shorebirds can leave as quickly as they need to, on a "hard weather migration." Both local and long-distance migrants move to the high Arctic in the spring, just ahead of a frozen world and sometimes dangerously with it, when there is little food. Sanderlings that migrate to the southern continent after their young are fledged will fly all the way to the southern coast of Argentina, a journey of some 8,000 miles. The well-publicized flight of another shorebird, the red knot, takes it 10,000 miles from the Arctic Circle to the tip of Tierra del Fuego. Some individuals may complete the trip in as little as thirteen days, though most take longer than that. In overcoming distance, these migrants rival the Arctic tern, which travels between the Arctic and the Antarctic each year, a round trip of up to 24,000 miles; but their performance is even more spectacular, since the tern travels at a far more leisurely pace, taking months to make the journey and feeding over the surface as it goes.

Brian Harrington of the Manomet Bird Observatory reported a ruddy turnstone that flew 2,750 miles from Alaska to an island in the Pacific in only four days. Subsequently, a semi-palmated sandpiper, shot on its arrival in Guyana, on the north coast of South

America, was found through the band on its leg to have been released at Plymouth Beach, Massachusetts, on August 12, 1985. It was picked up on the 16th, having flown 2,800 miles within those four days, to become the current champion, although this is not unusual. Shorebirds have been known to fly at heights of 10,000–20,000 feet on migration, and their speed has been timed at 40–50 miles an hour.

The truth is that no matter how fascinated we may be by the idea of record-breaking flights, they are not exceptional, but routine. It is not the individual shorebird, but the species that is capable of flying out from New England, nonstop across the waters of the North Atlantic, to reach the coast of South America. To accomplish this requires a massive consumption of energy. Individuals must have enough bodily reserves of fat so that they do not run out of energy during migration and perish.

The major feeding or staging areas, where many thousands of shorebirds congregate to fatten up during their migrations, are now few in number along the Atlantic seaboard, but they are vital to their future. Alternate sites have been lost to them, or further threatened by shorefront development and the destruction of wetlands. The toxic wastes, the herbicides and pesticides that continually wash out from the land and seep into remaining wetlands have unknown effects on their reproduction. Like other races, sanderlings have their "boom and bust" years, but it is estimated that their population has recently declined by 80 percent. This might in part be the result of chemical seepage in the river mouths and estuaries of Chile and Peru, where large numbers spend the winter.

Between the end of April and June, hordes of horseshoe crabs will lay their eggs on the shores of Delaware Bay, pulled in from deeper waters by moon tides which have been their signal for millions of years. In mid-May, between the 15th and the 20th, with a synchronized behavior that seems nothing short of miraculous if we were not aware of the beautifully timed and life-giving advents of the planet, thousands of red knots arrive to feed on this bounty.

The narrow strip of beach, extending for twenty miles along the shore, looks as if it were strewn with the litter and wreckage of combat. Thin-pointed spikes stick up out of the sand. Olive drab helmets lie out everywhere, many of them turned over, others half buried. Some are wedged between pilings that hold up the weathered beach cottages that stand over the beach. Through the murky brown waters just inshore, you can see these antediluvian animals, whose primitive eyes can only see changes between light and dark, as they wait to come in and mate. The males begin to arrive toward the latter part of April, and the females follow. Surges of egg laying along the coastline usually occur about two hours before high tide, and are inten sified by a full moon. These primordially slow creatures, if they are unable to get back to water on the ebb tide, bury into the sand and wait for high tide. Many pairs of males and females are still attached to each other. Horseshoe crabs lay eggs by the billion, by the ton, a productivity that does not in itself account for their survival. They have evolved relatively unchanged for 350 million years because of their adaptation to the consistently stable nature of the shallow seas on the rim of the continent.

Laughing gulls, many of them local nesters in the marshes behind the beach, are everywhere, wildly crying in a cacophonic chorus. They jostle each other, standing on the backs of the horseshoe crabs, and continually peck in the sand for eggs. Clouds of trim red knots, medium-sized shorebirds with robin-red breasts and silvery gray wings, come skimming in off the water, to land with a typically alert carriage on the beach. There they feed insatiably on the eggs, each egg being about the size of small black caviar. A considerable proportion of the knots have reached this haven of plenty, nonstop from Brazil, a distance of 8,000 miles. They have several thousand more miles to go in order to reach Victoria Island, their nesting grounds in the high Arctic. To fatten up for this migration, it is estimated that they will have to eat one egg every five seconds for fourteen hours a day, doubling their weight in two to three weeks' time.

At the least disturbance, the red knots spin off by the thousands over the water, then return to the beach, with that swinging unanimity common to shorebirds. When they finally reach Victoria Island, they nest secretly in the tundra, widely dispersed, often miles from each other. Without this feast of eggs, strategically located, the knots would have a difficult time surviving. The fact that petrochemical companies are located nearby gives the ornithologists a major cause for worry. One major spill could mean disaster for crabs and shorebirds.

An international effort is now under way to conserve and protect such staging areas, critical for some fifteen species of shorebirds on their migrations, and none too soon. The term "gluttony," sometimes applied to this temporary but intense period of feeding required to sustain birds on migration, is probably a misnomer. Gluttony might better describe industrial society. We consume a large part of the world's resources on such a scale as to become indifferent to what sustains us. Short-term profit threatens long-term starvation, not only of land and life, but of our own perception. A society unaware of its dependence on the rest of life has little to stop its almost unconscious greed but crisis. We now fall back on a world conscience which is in the throes of being born.

That sanderlings, sandpipers, or red knots, those little bundles of fat, muscle, and feathers, could accomplish such conquests of distance is awe-inspiring, although it is no less true of the ruby-throated hummingbird. Aside from explanations to do with its high metabolism and its breast muscles, can we really account for the fire in that tiny, atmospheric fish of a bird? This past autumn, I watched them feeding on the nectar of jewelweed along a shore in Nova Scotia, before they disappeared on their southward migration. They are jewels in themselves, carrying invisible engines of futurity. Regardless of how we rate them in terms of their significance, the universe fashions the smallest of living things with such craft as to meet its exalted and relentless standards.

Still, these birds are on a tightrope of survival. Their migrations are highly dangerous and often subject to severe cyclonic disturbances, driving them off course. Predators rob them on their territories of eggs and young. Food at the right time is critical; otherwise they are drained of their energy. They belong to one of the more fragile but enduring balances in nature, but their tenacity in following the earth's directions from pole to pole is a triumph in itself. There is a terrible discipline and urgency to these migrations, not unfamiliar to the history of human travel. Yet we do a great deal to shield ourselves from the kind of direct exposure experienced by the birds.

Blue sky and water days brighten the latter part of January, in between covering clouds, cold rain, and snow. A flock of about 150 sanderlings, with only a few dunlins, surprises me where I walk along the rim of the tide, landing only a few yards away, close enough for a quiet greeting. They hurry along, with that bright, crowd quickness of theirs. Then the whole flock lifts up and skims swiftly away, with a low crying that sounds like fine wires twanging in the wind. They are forever ahead of us. We only follow shorebirds to the shoreline.

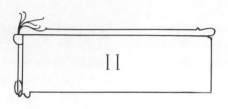

Global Wings

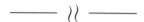

The open light, that perpetual summer which guides the life of terns and sanderlings, has not been absent from us, no matter how much we complain about winter days that hang in like a mortgage on the future. The sun rises a minute earlier than it did yesterday, and sets two minutes later. I am hardly aware of the change until it has progressed for many days but, in a global context, those three minutes must contain enough unseen dimensions and subtleties to occupy physics with a new theory of universal process. By the time the terns fly in from offshore, daylight will have lengthened by several hours, and it will be an occasion of great significance.

Every time I drive down to the shore, or drive to the town dump, I meet our resident gulls, whose gray and white plumage fits any kind of weather. All my life, I have watched them as they followed fishing boats and larger vessels wherever I traveled on Atlantic or European shores. Their cries rang out over the sound of human voices and the rattle and roar of machinery. They waited by docks littered with refuse, and tracked the wake of ships for fish remains and garbage. I followed their curved and sinewy wings under the blue sky, feeling that they had been there since the dawn of flight. I wonder if we did not learn to fly through watching them, lifted by the envy in our dreams.

Later on, I began to know gulls as scavengers and opportunists, as well as predators who would occasionally steal unguarded eggs and chicks, even of their own kind. They crowd by the thousands at city dumps. This might only remind you of centuries of beggars and outcast souls picking over the smoking wastes of civilization, but these are proud and handsome beggars, still independent, with their own music. They have aroused a great deal of resentment for crowding out tern colonies, getting in the way of airplanes, and letting their droppings fall on civilized roofs. At the same time, there is a kind of inadvertence in their behavior which seems familiar, as if both men and gulls had only learned through happenstance to follow what we think of as "progress." In a sense, they have been looking over our shoulders to steal the main chance. As a fellow "super-species" found over vast regions around the coasts of the world, they have learned how to take advantage of us.

Gulls and terns are relatives, with similar gray and white feathers for the most part (except for the black tern, and the noddy and sooty terns, whose plumage tends to shades of brown, black, and gray). The terns are more marine in their habits, fetching out farther over the seas. They are generally smaller, with forked tails and slender wings. They are highly coordinated in their constant over-water hovering and "plunge-diving" for fish, and their courtship flights are unparalleled in grace. They also bend to the power of ocean weather.

On the Maine coast, just after a minor hurricane, I watched some common terns flying inshore of stormy seas off Pemmaquid Point. They were in fast beating and, at the same time, twisting, bending flight, their long, pointed wings like thin, angled leaves tossed in a gale. The wind was blowing at thirty to forty miles an hour, and the terns would drop into the troughs of the waves to escape its full force and then lift again, making slow forward progress. The surface of the sea was full of green waves like a range of hills. Rocks, sea, and sky all glittered with the high glory of light a hurricane leaves behind it, while the surf boiled, roaring and rushing against the rocky shores, a massive amalgam of white and silver.

Terns, of which there are forty-two species, are worldwide in their distribution. Of these, twenty-two belong to the black-capped group called the Sterna, the variety commonly seen along the Atlantic shore from early spring to late summer. Not all terns are strictly confined to saltwater environments, nesting on islands, or on the sandy and rocky shores of the mainland. A number of them nest in both fresh and salt marshes. The black tern, which hawks for insects, breeds in shallow lakes and ponds, often making its nest in floating vegetation. Another of the marsh terns, the gull-billed, feeds on flying insects and land vertebrates, being partial to small fish, frogs, and tadpoles.

The common tern nests along the Atlantic shore as far south as the Carolinas, and across Canada to Newfoundland. It is also found in the Midwest, including the Great Lakes region, but is only seen off Pacific shores as a migrant. The least tern (little tern in Great Britain), of yellow bill and tinkling cry, nests along the upper part of sea beaches, where its eggs and newly hatched young are highly vulnerable to spring storms. Like the sanderlings and piping plovers, this very pleasing little bird has had a serious problem with human traffic, such as beach buggies, and barely endures an uneven competition for space with thousands of sun bathers during the summer months. The least has had similar problems in California, where it is an endangered species. It also nests on sandbars in the Mississippi, and has occupied spoil banks in disturbed areas. Showing a certain adaptability to suburbia, it has nested on rooftops in Florida, although the sloping, graveled roof of a supermarket may only wash its eggs down the drain during heavy showers.

Other terns are native to rivers in various parts of the world. They have similar ways of fishing, hovering over the surface with beaks pointed downward before they dive. Some "plunge-dive" into the water to catch their food, while others snatch it off the surface. Noddy, sooty, and fairy terns catch small fish out of the air as schools of them leap, or skip up to escape predators such as tuna. Many have a typically bouncy and, at the same time, deliberately stroking mode of flight. Being shallow divers, they are generally thin-plumaged, with little underdown. Unlike birds such as cormorants and auks, they are poor swimmers and cannot stand prolonged immersion. They like to stand offshore on floating debris or buoys, and are even seen on mats of seaweed or floating logs out in mid-ocean.

Most terns have similarly harsh cries, although the Peruvian tern, locally called *churi-churi,* is said to have a sweet, musical note, more like a shorebird's than a tern's. Many have forked tails, though some, like the common, Arctic, roseate, and royal, have tails that are more deeply indented than others, with long outer tail feathers called streamers. For this reason, many have been called sea swallows, especially those of the black-capped, gray-winged variety, although their flight, if highly maneuverable, does not have the quickly sailing and twisting ability of the swallows as they chase insects. I have seen common terns catch flying ants with considerable skill, but their ability to turn abruptly as swallows do is limited by their larger size.

The association of terns with swallows is not entirely a matter of forked tails. The black tern has a tail that is only slightly forked, but as it sweeps across inland marshes chasing insects, its flight looks very like a swallow's. (And, if only to indicate how form and function overlap in nature, there is a swallow-tailed, insect-eating shorebird called the pratincole, or swallow plover, of Asia and Africa. It flies with the grace of a tern, but also has a plover's characteristic way of running forward and stopping over open ground.)

The largest tern, the Caspian, with a blood-red bill, is about the size of ring-billed gull. Another large tern, though less heavy in appearance and flight, and with a more orange-shaded bill, is the royal. The robin-sized least tern is the smallest to be found along our shores. An even smaller one is the rare Damara, native to the southwest coast of Africa.

The genus *Sterna* includes the black-capped variety of terns. *Anous* is a genus heading for the noddies, found in tropical waters; and *Larosterna* is a monotypic genus comprising the Inca tern, an orna-

mental little bird found in the region of the Humboldt Current off
the west coast of South America. Inca terns have slate-gray feathers,
a dark red bill, and coral-red feet. They are adorned with a curving
white plume on each side of their head, extending below the eye.
They nest in cliffside burrows, an unusual habitat for terns, and in
flight they make quick swoops, fluttering and dashing over the surface of the sea, at times picking up fish almost out of the jaws of sea
lions as they come mouthing and snorting to the surface.

Harry Shapiro, the anthropologist, having just returned from an
expedition to the Pacific, once told me: "You should have been with
us when we were approaching the Marquesas in our ship. There
were hundreds of pure white fairy terns flying around and around,
with pearly translucent feathers which had a greenish cast because
of the waters reflected from below."

The fairy tern, one of the noddies, is found along the South Atlantic as well as the Pacific, breeding on small islands and wooded
mainland shores. Sometimes called white tern or Holy Ghost bird,
it is almost totally white except for its black eyes, which have a black
circle around them, making them look like disproportionately large
and shining pits. In the brilliant tropical sunlight, the bird's light
wings and body seem transparent, like "tiny flying skeletons" according
to Robert C. Murphy in his *Oceanic Birds of South America*. These
improbable little birds sometimes hover in the presence of human
beings, close enough to be picked up by hand. On one occasion,
they picked strips of fish bait off a man's arm. The fairy terns are
highly gregarious, keen-sighted birds that fly long distances out to
sea, hundreds of miles from their nesting islands, to hunt schools of
baitfish driven to the surface by tuna. When a flock discovers fish,
others are attracted from far and wide over the water. They serve
each other as beacons of oceanic light. Some flocks may contain
thousands of individuals, leaving nesting sites in the morning and
returning at dusk. They will also feed along the shoreline as the tide
comes in.

Fairy terns lay one egg, sometimes on a rock, but often on a branch,
where its balance seems to be in great jeopardy. All the same, eggs

and chicks seldom fall to the ground. I have heard that newcomers to the tropics are often offered bets on how long a fairy tern's egg will remain on some thin branch hanging in space. If they wager on a fall, they are bound to lose. The parent bird broods the egg in a semi-standing position, so as to shade it and keep it at the right temperature, at the same time clinging securely to its perch. The chicks are also equipped with strong claws that enable them to hang upside down by one foot if knocked over, and to swing back up again like acrobats.

Several million pelagic sooty terns, dark-winged birds of a more placid disposition than Arctics or commons, breed by the million in the Seychelles Islands of the Indian Ocean. The rest of the year their lives are spent on the wing over tropical seas. About one hundred thousand others inhabit the Dry Tortugas off the southern tip of Florida, where they nest on the ground. When John James Audubon, cruising among the Florida Keys in 1832, landed among the sooty terns, he felt that they would "raise me from the ground, so thick were they all around us, and so quick was the motion of their wings. Their cries were deafening."

Another famous colony of sooty terns, on Ascension Island in the mid-south Atlantic, is called Wideawake Fair because of the constant clamor of its population, night and day. In a scene out of *Oceanic Birds of South America* that seems approached as through a lens from the sky, its dense populations are described in this way:

> The site is well sheltered from the wind by hills and is very oppressive under the full blaze of the tropical sun, the more so because of an overpowering odor that arises from it during the time that the birds are present. The stench comes not alone from the guano but also from dead bones of young and adults and innumerable cracked and addled eggs, among which carrion beetles and their larvae swarm. From the slopes of Green Mountain, one can see the area as a greenish white patch, looking as though the bed of cinders had been whitened by a light fall of snow, while in the air above, the wheeling and hovering terns appear like a pillar of cloud that is never dissipated during the hours of daylight. The tremendous noise, which is so discordant and

ear-splitting at close range, blends in the distance to a sound like the murmuring of a vast crowd of human beings.

I have seen flocks of terns spread apart and come together in the shimmering air off the coast of West Africa. They rippled in the light over beaches by the Indian Ocean and scanned the surface of waters all gem blue and milky green, where fishermen in wooden dugouts with lateen sails moved in toward shore. They fluttered loosely in the distance over Lake Victoria. Some hawked for insects, while others dove into the shallow waters. I have watched African skimmers, allied to terns, as their strange, long, protruding mandibles sheared the surface of the river Nile, stirring up small fish. A flock of them rested on a sandbar. When our boat passed by, they rose off the bar and then returned to it, with dexterous strokes of their wings, as if they were patting the air.

Terns are part of the ancient breathing and abiding of the magnificent African continent. Their rhythmic behavior belongs to the ebb and flow of offshore tides, of grassland and bush, of drought, fire, and flood, of lakes with sodium-encrusted shores, heavy running rivers, warm seacoasts with sullen air, and mountains clothed in huge and shining leaves.

I have also watched the graceful, vehement Arctic terns as they dipped between the floating ice of Hudson Bay during the midnight radiance of late spring. Circle the world and you will find the terns ahead of you.

A line of thunderheads, like a succession of serial icebergs stood out to sea. The milky blue rollers flopped ashore, and there were flights of terns, skimming low over the bay, piercing the sound of the surf with thin metallic cries. ("Terns in Australia," in Bruce Chatwin, *The Songlines*).

Back on the winter shore, where the sanderlings fly off like little bullets for unknown destinations, I am momentarily carried with them, freed from the illusion that the human race has the world caged in. I cannot think of instinctive behavior in birds as foreign to me, when they have so sure a grasp of universality. They are not merely repeating involuntary actions when following their ancestral routes. They are earth's wings, and so outreach me. A seabird flies both for distance and the close at hand, bridging an unseen variety of ranges and conditions in between. So the dislodged feather I pick up off the beach, with its beautifully strong, light, and intricate construction, still carries an electric bond with the atmosphere. We own nothing that is more lasting. It reflects the endless transformations of those soft gray clouds lying over the horizon, and the running waves.

This beach I voyage on leads me through the earth's immortal consistencies. Each form I encounter obeys the principles of perfection and trial, a timelessness in the making. The proportions of truth are at hand. Existence is celebrated in a splinter of driftwood, worn by wind-driven sand into the shape of an arrow. The onshore waves jostle each other, busy with their eternal changing, mixing crab shells, sand grains, and fish bones together. The trim little shorebirds feeding at the water's edge are acutely aware of one another, under the light and shadow leaning and drifting over all awareness. With their own mysteries behind their beady eyes, their quick, advantageous movements, they follow the great, unifying sea.

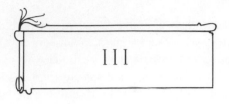

The Voice in the Name

The Forster's tern, another bird of the marshes, seems to float across them with effortless ease, looking very much like a common tern but with wings and tails of a paler gray. It was named by Thomas Nuttall in 1834 in honor of Johann Forster, a German naturalist. Trudeau's tern, a native of the interior marshes of Chile, Brazil, and Argentina, was named by John James Audubon for a friend of his, who had shown him an egg of that bird. The common tern by any lights is an uncommon bird, but gets its name from the fact of its worldwide distribution.

The word "tern" appears to have originated along the coasts of northern Europe, where people lived in a direct and intimate association with seabirds and the sea. For thousands of years, they had heard the cry of "keearrh" or "teearrh" from the common and Arctic terns, and there were a good many local names, now lost or no longer used, for these and other seabirds. There was such a wealth of common names, with varying pronunciations, from region to region, village to village, coast to coast, that it is often impossible to tell where they came from, or what they had specific reference to.

I once talked with Mrs. Edwin Muir, widow of the distinguished poet. She was brought up on an isolated island off the coast of Scotland. She spoke to me of oral tradition, the words and stories that come down "in the air" as she put it, translated electrically from generation to generation. A language and its names had the texture of local life. Before the industrial revolution started a world-wide process of displacement, the experience of living for so many centuries on an intimate basis with the land meant that each locality had its individual flavor and distinction. Variety flourished because the land itself was various.

Years ago, I also talked with a Maine lobsterman, who did not know what I was talking about when I asked him a question about terns. He finally decided that I was speaking of "medricks" which is a local name, along with "mackerel gulls" along that part of the coast and northward into Canada. The name seemed to suit the state of Maine, closer to Europe than any other—Maine with its monumental rocks walking and sliding into the sea, the saltwater brimming up through coves and islands for thousands of miles of intricate coastline. The summer waters were calm under light surface airs, but with sudden rushes and splashes through them like the presence of great fish. Cormorants riding the water dipped over and in quickly, with curving backs, and the lobsterman's kids did a little dance outside a gray shack perched on gray rock, storm-sanctioned, visited by mauve mists and lapped by tides a lichen-green. Crows of ragged wing drummed out harsh alarm calls: "Cadah! Cadah!" along the spruce-ranked shores behind them. When men, women, and children used speech that had evolved with the earth itself, their words followed a bird for a thousand years, walked the seasons, rowed in from the outhauls of the sea to an anchored, stony beach.

"Medrick," or a word somewhat like it, probably came from Europe, though there were other colloquial names for terns that sprang up after the settlement of the new world. Two of these for the least tern, which fit that attractive little bird very nicely, are "striking peter" in Florida, and "minner hawk" along the Mississippi and its tributaries.

"Paytrick," which may be allied with "medrick," is commonly used in Newfoundland, as well as "petrie," and both words may derive from a British folk name, "pickatiere" or "pickietar." "Piccatarne" and "pictarne" were used in the British Isles. An ancient British word *starn* is evidently the origin of a good many variants and is related to the Swedish *tarna* and Danish *terne,* as well as to the Norwegian *terna* and the French word *sterne.* The Spanish word is *charran.* Another Canadian name belonging to this company is *stearin.*

All these names must have originated in the cry of the bird, which sounds much the same in the common and the Arctic species, although the two have some distinctly different calls, and their voices differ in pitch, emphasis, and tone. In Europe, where both terns and swallows were found, there are equivalents of "sea swallow" in French *(hirondelle de mer),* Italian *(rondine de mar),* German *(seeschwalbe)* and Dutch *(zeezwalou).* The Welsh for sea swallow is *gwennol y mor.*

You can hear the cry of terns in old names such as "kip," "clet," and "rittoch." The big Caspian tern is known in Sweden as *skrantarne,* for its scream. "Screecher" or "screamer" has been used in the British Isles for several of the tern species. Another Scandinavian name is *ysgraell,* meaning "rattle," and a Welsh name for the Arctic tern is *ysgraell Gogledd,* or "northern rattle."

The terns, especially the commons, are also known in various parts of the world as mackerel gulls or mackerel terns because they often lead fishermen to the source of supply. The Japanese name for the common tern is *ajisashi,* or "horse-mackerel tosser"; for the least tern it is *ke-alji-sashi,* or "little horse-mackerel tosser."

In Portugal, a tern is a *gaivina,* and in the Cape Verde Islands, it is *garajau,* with a soft *g.* Cross the tern-traveled seas to Brazil and you will hear the common tern called *trinta reis,* and in some parts of South America a general name for terns is *gaviotin.*

The tern the North American Eskimo knows best is the Arctic,

and here again the cry of that bird is often reflected in the names
men have given it. Two of these, said to reflect the Arctic tern's
voice, are *tu-kuthl-kwi-uk* and *tiruyarak*. Another dialect name for
that species, which sounds to me when rapidly pronounced like the
staccato cry of a tern when attacking an intruder, is *ki-ti-ki-tee-ach*.
The Aleutian tern, common to Alaska, is called *chuf-chuf-chee-yuk*,
or *eg-lug-na-guk*, which refers to its white forehead.

I have been told by Dr. William S. Drury of the College of the
Atlantic, in Bar Harbor, Maine, that "the Eskimos at Eclipse Sound
said that their name for Arctic terns (which is the same as Alaskan
mitkotailyak and Greenland *immerquatailaq*) means that he walks on
his belly; i.e., has very short legs."

To a modern man accustomed to precise systems of classification
and nomenclature, Indian and Eskimo words for plants and animals
might seem vague and inaccurate but, in most cases, the opposite is
true. Their vocabulary is rich and their names subtle and descriptive. Names for plants and animals often refer to the kind of inconspicuous differences that most white men would not be aware of;
they do not classify, they describe, with the kind of detail that reflects
a close dependence. Native people were not only observers of what
we too quickly pass off as "nonhuman life," they knew themselves as
a part of it. They belonged to the same kingdom.

Indian and Eskimo names reflect the characteristics of the living
things they refer to, and often suggest a wide range of action. Among
the Chippewas, the Powatamis, and the Algonkians, almost uniformly, a bird was a *bineshi*, a bird in rapid flight was a *kikisse
bineshi*, and if it flew low to the ground, it was a *tabassisse bineshi*.
There were also qualifying terms for a small bird as well as a large
one, a bird with wings closed, and a bird hatched naked as distinguished from one hatched with feathers. The Massachusetts Indians
had a word for a single bird, for a number of birds, and for a little
bird *(psukses)*.

I find, incidentally, that the Crees, of Algonkian stock, still occupying large parts of Canada, refer to a tern as *keya'skoos*.

Without writing, scientific specimens, and the abstract relationships we depend on, Indians and Eskimos knew the birds extremely well. Individuals, as in all races, might differ in their ability to recognize one species from another, and some languages had more names for them than others, but they were able through memory and mutual association to transmit accurate characteristics of birds and consistent knowledge of them from generation to generation.

Their names for birds are often wonderfully descriptive and evocative. Through them, you hear and see the subject. One bird might be identified by its way of calling in flight and another by something distinctive in its appearance.

The Nunamiut Eskimos of the interior of Arctic Alaska called the young of the American gyrfalcon *atkuarvak*, which means "little caribou mittens." The red-breasted merganser was *akpaksruayood*, or "runs (like a man) on top of water." The northern short-eared owl was *nipailyntak*, or the "screecher"; the Baird's sandpiper was *nuvuksruk*, meaning "sounds like a man with a bad cold."

Clearly, such names come from a closer world, an intimacy with the land which in a great many regions is being swept away. The overpowering needs of civilization are driving out local identity. Native Americans, once on immemorial speaking terms with the birds through story, myth, and legend, "in the air," crossing the generations, now depend on alien power. Some have been able to adapt, others have lost their skills, and even their self-respect. When their language goes, so does their intimacy with nature, and the sacred knowledge of their Mother the Earth and their Father the Sun.

Still, the world of life does not change its speech and identities to suit our advantage. A true interpretation of any part of it depends on hearing the voice behind the name. Words, in this utilitarian age, may seem to turn into loose change, the debased coin of the realm, but that resonant cry of the tern is a signal of what lasts. "Keearrh!" comes down unchanged out of an ageless past, like frogs still sounding their "rek-rek," or the "coax-coax" of the frog chorus in Aristophanes. These are cries that communicate the basic identity of a race; and they carry ancient seas and island roots down to the present, with unalterable distinction.

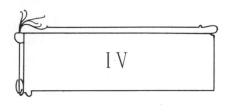

Life Lines and Sea Lanes

The sun shines through the gull-gray clouds like yellow crystal. A flock of several hundred shorebirds reappears, skimming low over the water like a sparkling wheel. Having weathered one stormy shore, these tough little birds move on to another. Winter storms batter the coast, bringing down cliffs and breaking through barrier beaches, insisting on their superior, time-honored right to change. Storms dignify our lives if only because we are unable to avoid them. They put us in touch with continental dimensions.

Tidal New England country, on the forefront of weather from all parts of North America, waits through frozen and thawing days. Icy rain spits and scatters through the trees and across the marshes. On days of very hard cold, shallow pools of water look like congealed sheets of mercury. Out on the marsh, a few Canada geese stand and watch, or stalk over the ground with a dignified, rolling gait, while the omnipresent gulls cruise by in the chilly air. A travel readiness is in the birds, at all times of the year.

I can see some draggers out in the distance, working hard through

rough seas to overcome a drastic decline in the supply of fish. Otherwise, the trials of the sea have become distant from our experience, and in a relatively short time. I think of those voyages of the past as they crossed the trackless ocean, over the monotonous rolling of the waves. These were human migrations that endured great privation, were often disastrous and, at the same time, passionately sought after. Though its expectations may have been shorter then, life was no less desirous:

> The man knows not, prosperous being, what some of those endure who most widely pace the paths of exile. And yet my heart is now restless in my breast, my mind is with the sea-flood over the whale's domain; it fares widely over the face of the earth, comes again to me eager and unsatisfied; the lone-flier screams, resistlessly urges the heart to the whale-way over the stretch of the seas.
>
> The hail flew in showers. I heard naught there save the sea booming, the ice-cold billow, at times the song of the swan. I took my gladness in the cry of the gannet and the sound of the curlew instead of the laughter of men, in the screaming gull instead of the drink of mead. There storms beat upon the rocky cliffs; there the tern with icy feathers answered them. (From the Anglo-Saxon poem, *The Seafarer*)

As knowing instruments, the "icy-feathered" terns, quite possibly the Arctic terns, are far better at interpreting the distances they travel than are any of those machines that take us wherever we want to go. When they come in out of the sea, it is as if they were on magic wings out of a mythical age, but they are ancient and confident residents of a wilderness we are beginning to regret and wish we had known better, now that we are leaving it behind.

An ornithologist companion on a trip to Denmark, who had been an underground resistance fighter against the Germans during World War II, made the remark that terns do not respect national boundaries. Nor did the Lapps who used to wander with their reindeer over the hills and mountains of Norway, Sweden, and Finland. But their ancient migrations had been cut off in modern times as a result of long borders guarded by sentries, barbed wire, and intersecting searchlights. Conquering space and all earth barriers to progress has not spared us our imprisonments. The long-distance migration of seabirds and other animals has always been full of risk, but it shows . an instinctive mastery of direction, and an enviable freedom.

As Donald Griffin pointed out in *Bird Migration:* "The maximum extent of bird migration is limited not only by the capabilities of the birds, but by the size of the planet." Is it surprising that human longing should have attached itself to birds?

Except for the season when they come in to breed and nest on islands or such beaches as are still open to them, terns can spend long periods of time on the wing. They are great wanderers, having traveled the seas and the rims of the continents for millions of years. The terns that land on our shores are notoriously unstable, with a nervous fear of being confined to any one place. It is always imperative that they be able to move to alternate sites when the local food supply fails them, or a habitat is denied them.

Seabirds that travel the open ocean, such as Wilson's petrels, greater shearwaters and long-tailed jaegers, are often lost to sight. They can be studied seasonally, because they return to breeding sites where they can be watched and banded, but after they leave the land, their movements are almost impossible to trace. They simply disappear into the oceans of the hemisphere. Satellites are now being used to trace whales, as well as schools of fish, not, one hopes, to their detriment. They may soon be able to track down far-ranging and elusive seabirds as well. Such investigations might help lead the way toward a more open world than the one we have been imposing on the earth's environment. Still, these outer, borrowed eyes can never see far enough without a corresponding inner vision which we can share with birds.

The Arctic tern has a coastal, 'round the world route that is better known. It breeds by the hundreds of thousands in a range extending across northern Alaska and Canada, Greenland, Iceland, northern Europe, and Asia. After the nesting season, these fabulous travelers fly down two main migratory routes, one along the continental shelf of western Europe, passing the coast of Africa, and the other down

the Pacific coasts of North and South America. The majority appear
to fly as far as the rim of the Antarctic pack ice, where they spend
the winter resting on ice floes, and feeding on krill in the leads and
openings between them.

On their autumn migration, Arctic terns crossing the Atlantic are
probably helped by favorable winds. Then they fly down the coasts
of Europe and Africa in a deliberate way, hovering and diving for
food as they go. When they reach South Africa, they have largely
used up their physical resources, while the journey ahead, across
hundreds of miles of stormy seas to the Antarctic, is the hardest yet.
Still, it is supposed that they travel fast on their final lap, resting
only briefly on scattered icebergs and occasional islands along the
way. This is a region of strong winds and heavy gales, but the flight
of terns is bending and flexible, and they are able to ride the winds
and keep their general heading.

An Arctic tern may journey up to 12,000 miles one way. This
species evidently experiences more daylight than any other bird on
earth, because of a breeding season that takes it to northern latitudes
where the sun rarely sets, and a migration to wintering grounds
where there are only short hours of darkness. That the two polar
extremes should be so lodged in their minds that they have no more
problem in navigating between them than we do in getting home
from work seems like an amazing feat. Yet their kind has been following this global map for time out of mind, adjusting to its changes
for thousands of years, with audacity, deliberation, and innate skill.

It is puzzling that most, if not all, of these migrants, though living
on the wing for much of their lives, and accustomed to wander,
should need to go as far as the Antarctic during the winter months.
There are rich, winter feeding grounds much closer to where they
nest. Perhaps, it is thought, they may have originated in the Antarctic, and have a genetic memory that pulls them back. Why, also,
do they not stop off the coast of Africa, to winter there? From a long-
range perspective, which is the best way to view an Arctic tern, it is
very much to their advantage. Their migration reaches a far northern
spring when it is fairly exploding with new sources of food and

energy. The return journey heads for a southern summer, where the upwelling of deep waters around the immense polar continent also produces a great abundance of food.

Depending on what kinds of food they eat, the terns, or any other widely dispersed birds of the sea, reveal what lies beneath the surface waters, largely hidden to us. They are dependent on the vast, fluid energies of water masses and their convergences, on the upwellings and downsinkings that effect the periodic abundance or dearth of plankton, and on the movements of ocean currents that shift the food supply. Birds unable to keep up with such changes die. Their life lines are the sea lanes of the world.

Seabird migrations are controlled first and foremost by the light and heat of the sun, as it affects climatic zones and atmospheric conditions, linked in turn with the circulation of ocean waters. The various environments of the world ocean range from rich feeding areas to near deserts. The highly salty Mediterranean supports relatively few seabirds. There are also impoverished regions in the subtropics, whose warm and salty waters lack the wealth of plankton found in Antarctic seas, or off the Grand Bank of the North Atlantic, where many thousands of seabirds gather to feast. Seabirds are dynamic travelers, on the lookout for food over the vast ranges between the poles.

(Along the Atlantic coast of America, we are more likely to see the common tern than the Arctic, which is now rare in its southernmost range of Massachusetts, but nests along the Maine coast and up into far northern Canada. It looks very much like the common tern, but its beak is all crimson in the breeding season, instead of red with a black tip. The Arctic also has shorter legs, and a voice with a shriller pitch to it. Its tail feathers are longer, but both species share black caps and slender, gray wings, plus a pugnacious disposition when defending their nests, suggesting an evolutionary history full of predators.)

The Arctic tern's migration comes full circle around the world, having accommodated to ages of planetary movement. The appropriate territories each migrant species explores for food and breeding sites are as shifting in their nature as the weather, from season to season, day to day. Animals, especially the free flying birds, have to be flexible to meet the unexpected. The characteristic patterns of bird migration that exist today may have evolved during the last ice age, which melted back some 15,000 years ago. This suggests an innate ability to adapt to earth changes over a relatively short period. Behind that, of course, lie hundreds of millions of years in which the continents drifted apart and ice ages moved in and retreated with a monumental, graduated rhythm. Some persistent migratory routes, like those of the sea turtles in the South Atlantic, may have been a lasting response to some drastic shift in the earth's crust which cannot be traced. The consistencies science looks for in trying to understand migration have all time behind them.

The unchanging rhythm of night and day, the rolling beat of the tides, in and out like our own breath, is eternally reassuring. At the same time, we are born with a restlessness which is as close to fundamental nature as any of our ideas about it. We reflect a planet that is never at rest. We respond to its daily moods, its often violent extremes, with passionate uncertainty, always searching for solutions to an inner hunger we are unable to control.

On this winter day, the sun still hangs low in the sky. Its light glitters on every grain of sand, and outlines each black rock and water-dark stone along the beach in stark detail. It is carried on the backs of the gulls and burns on the whiteness of the new sea ice now beginning to pack in along the shore, after two days and nights of temperatures well below freezing. And it levels out over the entirety of the seas, a dazzling reach that blinds the vision.

In the uncompromising country farther north, when the snow lies so deep that deer struggle to find enough browse, they may travel slowly, aimlessly, half-starved, until winter finally blinds and shatters them. Looking out is almost an act of desperation at times, but looking out is basic to the life of shorebirds, or to an Arctic tern as it flies with the revolutions of the earth against the sun. This has as much to do with life's vitality of spirit as it does with predictable behavior.

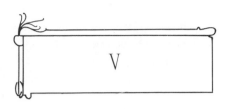

Timing

I timed a week or more of the month in November, as it was changing toward colder days, by the great flinging falls of the gannets migrating from Canada. Out over the bay, the dark-plumaged young and the adults like pure white cloud islands shining in the light were following schools of fish. They wheeled over the water from high in the air while individuals suddenly pitched down in with superbly controlled abandon. They signaled a moving over to another phase of the year, with a style our literal calendars are unable to match.

There are also sporadic events in the local weather which are so unexpected and dramatic that I know I have watched a pivotal moment in the year. April may be announced by no more than a single cloud, founded in a depth of complexity beyond deciphering.

A great barreling cloud, many miles long, hangs over the sea parallel to the shore, ending in a dark funnel in the distance. The waters are still and calm, breathing easy, with a few gulls riding on the surface. Suddenly, an east wind moves in with a roar, changing this flat table into shivered silver, then kicking up small waves, a grizzled-green. In a few moments, the cloud is totally dispersed into the western sky over the land. The wind has blown everything in waiting somewhere else, into a new phase of experience. The spontaneous ones in the life of earth ride with its energies, circle, pivot, balance, and move on.

The island at the edge of the marsh, where the terns nested last year, lies under the sky like a receptive lens, having some of the transforming qualities of the waters that surround it. The marshes themselves go on rising and sinking with the invading and retreating tides. Where I leave them, to walk over the sand dunes, on higher ground, a cloud of short-lived, tiny flies catches my eye. Then I find a fox scat with mice hairs in it, and a brown and white roll of fur, the last of a cottontail. So I am centered in mutability, within the constancy of the seasons.

I have no reason to go to Florida in order to escape the weather. I would only find it there ahead of me. This is certainly not the way of the sparrow, hopping into view out of the reeds along the salt marsh channel. Its distinction was born in the place which was allowed its own identity, beyond good, bad, or inconvenient.

Out of the land, there is a mutually engendered electricity between the sunlight and the bare trees, as they shake in a chilly wind. I am unable to see the process, but I know that their twigs and branches, and the leaf buds with their inner-sprung intentions, must begin to stir in the weeks ahead in response to a changing chemistry. Trees are chronometers of life's weather, which moves according to the intelligence of the universe.

As a society that imposes grids and dams on the free flowing earth, and counts on speed for its communication, we disguise these passages of light. In the process of our moving out from where we are, time becomes our exclusive property, though we ought not to assume that the birds do not have some sense of it too. The imposition of Standard and Daylight Time cheats us into believing that we are time's masters and manipulators, but it is only the sun that centers us. Catch the light if you dare. It is a truth that brings all things into question.

When the periwinkles begin to make their coiling, meandering tracks over the tidal sands, I can attribute it to shores now free of ice and below freezing temperatures, though the waters offshore are never entirely without food. Beginning as early as February, and on through March, along with an upwelling of waters rich in nitrates and sulfates, the light increases in intensity and penetrates the coastal seas. Phytoplankton surges in response. Microscopic, glassily encased diatoms increase at such a fantastic rate as to change the color of the water. The tiny animals of the plankton, the pulsing, whirring drifters, also increase with the intensifying radiation from the sun and graze on the plant life. Except for the greening of the waters, they are largely unseen by most of us, but these multitudes of global food sustain the life of the seas, the planet, and ourselves.

A few years ago, I saw a wide, reddish band of copepods strewn along a white beach on one of the Falkland Islands, a few hundred miles north of the Antarctic Circle. The sea just offshore was clouded with them, and they had been washed in by the tides. Each of these small creatures, rowers with oarlike feet and orange-scarlet, nearly transparent bodies, glowed in the light like tiny meteors. Their black eyes, an impenetrable speck in their heads, were made of the sea's black soundings and the prisms of the sky. They are short of life and quick to die, of a sensitivity as fine as a touch of air on a sunlit tidepool. If enough of them, and the uncountable members of the plankton, could no longer survive because of a drastic change in their environment, the whole earth would be subjected to an instability that could threaten existence. Plankton is the world's food, and the damage unbridled industrial expansion has already done to the atmosphere now threatens it beyond recall. The ozone layer, over the Antarctic and the Northern Hemisphere, is turning into vast, seasonal holes, as the chemistry of the upper atmosphere starts to break down. An increase in ultraviolet light by a mere 5 percent could cut the life span of the sea's micro-organisms in half, with disastrous, proliferating effects on the earth's ecosystems and its climate. We outsize predators have run through whole continents with an ignorance of the destruction we bring upon them.

The light of copepods mediates between sea and sky, and burns for a future that men threaten to foreclose. Pascal was terrified by the infinite spaces of the universe. I am terrified by how much we fail them.

The spring graduates its appearances, and at the same time expresses an often violent inconsistency. Tornadoes, storms of snow, hail, and ice, winds of hurricane intensity, widespread flooding, wreck the mainland. Nothing is born without passion, and life responds on time. Flocks of male redwings fly in the first week in March, then a small school of migratory alewives shows up in the local brook. A few weeks later, spring peepers, the hyla crucifer, cry out from the bogs with such a shrill intensity as to crack the starlight. Once I took the family dog down to a nearby hollow known as Berry's Hole. It was after dark and the wind was shaking the still leafless trees while moonlight leaked in through slowly crossing clouds. A high-pitched, scratchy warbling rose up as we came near, and then a scattered belling and tinkling, followed by silence, and then another wave of choiring. The dog whimpered at first and, when we reached the edge of the hollow, began acting wildly. The wind shook the trees and the moon's reflection danced on their trunks and branches and over pools of water in the bog, while the hylas throbbed and called. The dog seemed to find it an experience he was unable to sort out and kept frantically running around, stopping, whimpering, barking crazily. With our separate endowments, I could find it exalting, and the dog hair raising, but we were both responding to one of the ancient rituals of the earth, perpetually wild, and open to all the senses born to hear it.

The spring peepers do us a profoundly important service, which as mere landowners we are unaware of. To bury their habitat, to poison and pollute it so that these tiny tree frogs no longer proclaim their mating rites but inherit a dead world, is to destroy the distinction of a place. If they disappear because of us, the silence will be deafening. We will not know where we are.

The temperature is at the freezing point again, and wet snow falls, while the small, tight buds of the wild cherries begin to be tipped with green. The buds on the oaks are hard and brown, slow to respond. Mourning cloak butterflies, released from hibernation on bright, warm days, disappear when it clouds over. Later on, little spring azures—"powder blue" butterflies—follow, flitting low over the ground. They feed on the small, early flowers of the ground-hugging bearberry, or "hog cranberry," plants. These are the local accents of response to a tempered extravagance that colors the earth. Each life responds on time, according to the triangulations of the sun between one pole and the other. In a world made smaller by human dominance, the butterflies of spring keep me in touch with the planet's abiding distances.

All things are now at risk. All things are at risk in being reborn. We are not the ones who build the future. Each small existence, spanning the gap between the unconscious depths and the rising into the light, is sent on by an immortal hunger. Each of them climbs Mount Everest all the time.

When the stars of April dive down into the sea, all associations, human or nonhuman, come together. The gulls that are standing around the horizon, or lifting down the shore, seem to cry out more musically than usual. When they are backlit by gray clouds and a westward trending sun, they glint like mica. The massive coastal waters run under the changing animal light, opaque, gray-green, shining like a knife, dull as a stone. The nature of these ocean waters merges with the shores they touch. When the terns come in to nest at the end of the month, or in early May, some choose areas where flood tides and spring storms can destroy their eggs and chicks. It is a world of continuous physiographic changes, with a movable and inconsistent food supply, such as the small fish the terns feed on.

The tidal grounds are unrelenting in their demands on crabs, sea worms, sand shrimp, barnacles, shellfish, and a great many other forms of life, each with its protective devices against what assails them. Winter ice and below freezing temperatures devastate great numbers of them. During the hot months, many have to endure alternate tidal flooding and periods of exposure to the desiccating sunlight. The relative salinity of the water changes; temperatures fluctuate, often drastically; populations die out or move from one location to another in response to changing conditions; storm waves tear at their hold on the subsurface. But this protean environment describes the floods of life itself, the mercurial energies that run through all forms of creation. We too are creatures of water's genius, and can never substitute for it.

The alewives, freshwater herring, begin to head in to an inlet that leads through the marshes, joining a creek that threads its way down from the upland ponds where they spawn. At mid-tide, where salt-water meets fresh, the herring gulls wheel over them, crying out triumphantly like the horse in the book of Job:

> He saith among the trumpets,
> Ha, ha: and he
> Smelleth the battle afar off.

When one of them plucks a fish of flat and shining silver out of the stream, others lunge and scramble after it like footballers piling in on the ball carrier.

Farther down the shore, bold, hoarse and croupy-voiced black-backs, considerably larger than herring gulls, have been attacking skates in the shallow waters at the edge of the tide. In death, the fins of these fish curl up stiffly around their flat, speckled bodies, and their slick, startlingly white underbellies have markings on them like little pug faces, with two holes and a slit of a mouth.

The gulls were few in number in the Northeast at the beginning of the century, but quickly took advantage of the vast supply of waste that accumulated with the spread of cities and offshore fishing fleets. Their population grew by leaps and bounds, from a few thousand to hundreds of thousands. Gulls will eat almost anything. This has enabled them to bypass those natural seasons of privation when the young had to fend for themselves and often starved to death in their first winter. Modern recycling centers, where it is much harder for them to reach food, are now contributing to a marked decline in the gull population, but they are still very much in evidence. Gulls are animals of a predatory world that moves in whenever it sees an opening.

Gulls have been forcing their light and buoyant relatives, the terns, out of their habitats, with considerable help from us. Terns are opportunistic too, so far as their food and nesting territories are concerned, but not on the same order of magnitude.

The gulls are with us, come what may, and I should miss them if they were not. They are tough survivors and scavengers, standing in with the enduring weather, knowing they are as much a part of the coastal seas as the waves curling along the beaches. I suspect they see more than we do, who try to occupy these continental shores on our own terms. Life-giving perceptions of land and water pass us by, while the gulls keep their signals intact. They are continually paying attention, while we are looking in some other direction. It amounts to an alarmingly short attention span, as compared to a watchfulness in tune with a thousand years.

I am continually missing out on the events, the rituals and ceremonies now taking place in the living world. All the same, no matter how disengaged or unpracticed in seeing I may be, I walk with the earth, I breathe its air, and I can never abandon its stirrings in my being. The spring rocks new life out of me and I call back to it out of reaches I have never fully realized. With those birds now singing: "Here! Here!" I am challenged once again to equate myself with "all that's made."

Thunder and lightning bowl in out of the alleys of the sky, and a powerful wind drives sheets of snow across the sands. When it clears, gray fog covers the shore with half a sun burning through it; gases bubble up through marsh peat and slick mud where mud snails cluster and crawl, and the minnows wiggle at low tide. Further inland, the warm sunlight softens the ground for fissures made by worms and nematodes, and runs through the cellular passages of the frogs. Lightly dancing flies make shadows over dead leaves. Each tribe in its time, each inhabitant of every inch of wet or dry ground, counts what is countless through its awakening.

All through the tidelands and between the island grasses, the oaks and the pines, birds display or, like Canada geese, fly up and vee off on major journeys. Under the clatter and roar of machinery, even under our sealing over of the ground, life moves up like the mushrooms I have seen shouldering through a load of asphalt to claim the light. I do not know what kind of a being man is, to be able to leave the planet behind him, as if to improve on the birds, but he is still moved by thunder and the April surf, and he is unwittingly sensitive to the air and water that created him. We are angered and embattled; we hope and pray; we fall out of the flock and vanish, not because of anything we can do on our own, but because we are sent ahead by the same subterranean reality as anenomes in a tide pool, or caribou on migration. A greater timing, never to be overtaken by mathematics, is what revolutionizes being.

The Arrival

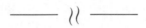

The season advances not so much in terms of fixed dates as in waves, which may be the best way to understand the mind of a bird. By mid-April, there are bands of green bloom in the offshore waters of Cape Cod Bay and, along the Outer Beach, the great green cylinders boom and crash as they lose momentum, one behind the other, ending in sheets of foam that sink into the sloping sands. Early arrivals, the graceful laughing gulls, with black heads and slate-gray wings, hover over the shoreline, dipping down into the breaking waves, where they pick up bits of food. They have migrated from coastal regions in the southern state where they have spent the winter, while thousands of locally wintering waterfowl get ready to move out.

Winter to spring—spring to winter—come together in the various migratory impulses of the birds, spanning the hemispheres. In this latitude, the first day of spring comes on March 21, which is the first day of winter in countries many thousands of miles to the south of us. In the open seas off Patagonia, petrels and albatrosses perpetually scan the waters, often in the teeth of gale winds, and the Antarctic and South American terns skim between the islands of the archipelagos that lead down to the Antarctic continent. From one end of the earth to the other, crossing the seasons, the seabirds roam, following its energies and its food. They were exploring the world ocean long before man set out to voyage beyond the known horizon.

Different races of birds have been described as being slaves to their particular forms of environment and their food, but they are highly accomplished in their employment of them, and they are also outreachers on a global scale. It would be to our benefit if we followed them, as initiates in the ways of a far more intricate world than we can possibly grasp on our own.

Last year, toward the end of April, I was a little late, according to their schedule, in putting up bird houses for the tree swallows. They had arrived ahead of me. As I was busy nailing a house to its post, a white-bellied, iridescent-winged swallow suddenly materialized, fluttering to within a few inches of my head. "Get on with it," it seemed to say, "where have you been all this time?"

There are wonderful occasions, in the absence of that literalism that plagues us so—"What does it do?" "What good is it?" and so on—when human beings and wild birds may meet in something like a conversation. At least we attend to one another on the basis of expectation, watching and listening. It has always given me great pleasure to listen to swallows, barn or tree, as they lightly, gently twittered, like a string of water beads. This singing speech is often hard to interpret in any satisfactory way, and much of it goes beyond our range of hearing, but it comes in to us as an earth music in which we have always found companionship.

An Arctic tern, having flown to the Antarctic and back in the same year, may return to a nesting site within a few meters, or even inches, of where it nested the previous year. Other seabirds, such as petrels, will return to the exact same burrow on a seaside cliff. A robin comes back to build its nest in the shrub near my house, while a phoebe nests again in the eaves. Alan Poole, who has written a definitive book on the osprey,* points out that individual, marked ospreys use the same nest year after year, wintering along the Amazon and returning to the coast of New England. This is what the ornithologists call site tenacity, or site fidelity. That birds can accomplish such accurate travel over very long distances implies a sophisticated system of navigation, and an insistence in them, such as my tree swallow displayed, that comes from knowing where they are headed. Their routes have been extensively mapped through radar tracking and scientific teams, but the amount of knowledge needed to understand this worldwide phenomenon as a whole, or in detail, is still beyond us. The earth, as I can see, even when I walk out on a sea-washed beach, is completely covered by the tracks of living communities that follow the land, the waters, and the atmosphere, in often painstaking detail. I am only concentrating on one kind of life at the moment, and I know little enough of that. Still, if I stay in one place long enough, I may be able to glimpse the unity which holds all tracks together.

Waiting for the terns to come in involves me in the practice of looking out, and measuring the passage of time in terms of the light, the wind, and passing clouds, as compared to the news that tells me nothing but that time begins and ends on the day I hear it. It is the birds who are in charge of the future.

The local world lies open and clear after another cold April storm. Big, steely clouds drift slowly over the sea, blindingly blue Mediterraneans appearing between them. The tide moves out, while tier after tier of low white waves rush in against the wind. The weight of the ocean beyond me tugs at my senses, pulling me out. If I could fly up over the shore with those easy-riding gulls, feeling the tension of distance, I might learn to explore the wide world with more confidence.

On a clear, spring night, migratory birds can be seen hurrying across the surface of the full moon. Some species can be identified with a pair of field glasses, and their relative numbers estimated.

*Alan F. Poole, *Ospreys,* Cambridge University Press, 1989.

The flow of migration across those clear skyways is one of the wonders of the world, like the moon itself, which still retains its mysterious, tide-raising light, in spite of our claims to landing rights.

Terns flying north arrive when there is a ready supply of fish ahead of them, as if they knew that they would be there, and it is quite likely that they do. After all, they follow the annual change in the earth's relationship to the sun. They accommodate seasonal revolutions in the sea and in the atmosphere. Moon tides, which stimulate marine creatures to feed and spawn, may pull at their senses. Terns may also have an awareness of the difference in time between unfamiliar terrain and their breeding territories. There is a hemispheric timing in their being. They take on worlds of direction which we have hardly begun to recognize.

The terns beat their way north from the southern continent in relatively small groups of a hundred or so, arriving at their nesting grounds in progressive waves. Normally, they begin to show up off southern New England in late April, or early May. Over an island that may be miles out to sea, on overcast days especially, the terns may be heard before they are seen. They fly high overhead as if flirting with the place they have flown thousands of miles to reach. Fishermen are likely to spot them days before they finally settle down for good on their nesting islands. One year, I heard of two pairs being sighted offshore along the coast of New Jersey about April 10, and a number off Cape Cod the third week in April.

Those returning to a site where they have successfully bred the year before feel a strong compulsion to return to it. Evidently, these early arrivals stimulate later birds to move in. Already mated birds often arrive earlier than two-year-old, unmated birds. Juveniles in their first year, not physically ready to breed, may not migrate at all, but stay where they are, along the coasts of South or Central America.

The contrast between their wintering grounds and the coastline of the North Atlantic could hardly be greater. The terns leave thousands of miles of the low-lying, hot, and sultry shores of a continent threaded with great rivers and innumerable tributary estuaries and lagoons. The mudflats are often vast in extent, especially along the northern coast of South America, where there are few, if any, beaches, and there is only a small tidal flux. The big, muddy rivers disgorge uprooted trees, which float out to sea, a half-sunken hazard for vessels, but fine roosts for the terns, whose small pearly bodies can be seen lined up along them like strings of beads. They feed offshore by day and roost along the coast at night, where they are in some danger of being trapped by local people for the market.

The nights, along this great coastline, from the Caribbean southward, are magnificent with their thick cover of brilliant stars. The sun shines fiercely by day. The rains, copious in season, deliver varying amounts of moisture during the rest of the year to a continent of abundant water.

The terns' breeding range in the north, on the other hand, is characterized by often heavily forested shores, rocky islands, sandy and gravelly beaches, while warm currents and cold waters merge and mix over the continental shelf. The tidal range is extreme, between forty and fifty feet in the northern reaches of the Bay of Fundy to only two feet to the south of Cape Cod. During the winter, most fish have moved out to deeper, ice-free water, but during the transformations of late winter and early spring, the offshore waters begin to have an abundance of the small fishes the terns depend on. These long-distance migrants respond to the rhythms of two distinct and majestic coastlines, joined by the roaming food of the seas.

For many of the adults, there may be a certain amount of searching between alternate sites before they settle in to nest. In spite of their consistent faithfulness to particular territories, year after year, terns depend on a coastal environment which can be as changing and as volatile as their own natures. Even after a colony has moved in and started to pair up and establish nests, the birds may desert and settle somewhere else because of predators, a failure in the local supply of fish, or severe disturbance of their habitat. If the move is made early enough in the season, they must have alternate sites to move to, and these are becoming scarce on these crowded shores. (Even under favorable conditions, populations of terns are generally unstable, fluctuating, moving up and down over the years. They belong to a world of movement, in which instability and the unpredictable are commonplace.)

The terns, of course, never had any alternative but to risk the odds that face them. They are intense, resilient little birds, built to meet adversity and attrition, although they have never had to face the pressures of human growth on its present scale. Their migration still follows original space, out of a deep, wild past which they measure with confidence, as if in defiance of our neglect of it.

A cold, raw wind blows hard along the shore. Weeks of unusually cold April weather have held back the inland schooling of the alewives. Normally, great numbers of these fish will have long since pressed in through the salt marshes to head up for the freshwater ponds where they spawn. They have been coming in since March, but only in small schools. On any average year, the big runs occur by at least mid-April. These fish are acutely sensitive to temperature, swimming inland when the freshwater streams are warmer, if only by a few degrees, than the saltwater at their outlets. The shad, or shadblow, with its light gray, lichen-spotted trunks, has been slow to flower. The tree swallows have been delayed.

Day after day, I look out from the shore for incoming terns, even when I know it is too early. Perhaps they will never appear; perhaps the weather is too cold and rough for them, and they will be abnormally late. That insularity of mind and spirit which keeps us separated from real progress, the fundamental rhythms of the earth, makes us worry about obstacles that may not exist. The terns will not fail to appear simply because I find it colder than usual, or because I am unable to see beyond the immediate horizon. All the same, I know that the relatively small marsh colony at Gray's Beach has been severely dropping in numbers in recent years, and I cannot be sure of them in a way I had once hoped to be.

May the 2nd, and the temperature goes below freezing at night, and hovers at 40° Fahrenheit during the day. The wind buffets the coastline, as heavy, cloud curtains hang over the marine horizon. Many ducks and geese have moved further inshore and ride on the relatively protected waters at the mouth of the broad inlet, or tidal creek, that borders one edge of the salt marsh. A slender yellowlegs, a new arrival, slants up against the wind with a piercing whistle, then flies off to land on a more sheltered level of the marsh. I look out over the water, but the terns are nowhere to be seen.

Terns are fast, tireless flyers, and it would not take them long to fly nonstop from South America to these shores. But unlike the shorebirds, they have a step-by-step migration. Shorebirds travel on fat stored up during their intense feeding at a few sites, or "staging areas," whereas the terns do not have that capacity, and pick up fish as they go. With their flexible, deliberate wing beats, they fly fairly low over the water, not up to 20,000 feet as some shorebirds do, and they bend to varying weather conditions on their way.

At last, after a few bright, warm days, the alewives begin to move in, in greater numbers, with the yellow-beaked gulls, their plumage as clean as a clam shell, screaming over them, plucking them out of the shallow stream. Where the fish are concentrated in fish ladders and resting pools below their spawning grounds, they are packed in so thickly together that they lack oxygen, sliding past each other on their gleaming sides, making quick gulps at the surface.

Children along the banks of our local herring brook try to catch these slippery migrants from the sea with their hands. The alewives leap ahead like a pulse. The girls scream and the boys yell whenever they catch one and their wet hands shiver as they try to hold it, violently struggling, gasping for air. Nature meets with nature. They scream with the silver fire in their hands because it is strange, and because they cannot let it go.

The season tides ahead with the same power and inevitability I see reflected in the big, round, and lidless eyes of an alewife. A greening deepens on the marshes. A neat, quick little warbler flies in to show me that there are still some forests left in Central America. Finally, on the 8th of May, I hear the ratchety, grating, exhilarating cry of a tern piercing the fog that hangs in like a wall, a hundred yards offshore, and I call out in welcome to it.

The following day, a few terns are flying down the tidal creek on the edge of the marsh at Gray's Beach, and a group of forty is lined up on a sandbar at the mouth, perfectly spaced, a forward-looking, wind-facing phalanx. I notice one or two craning their heads and necks toward the sky, a hint of more intense mating behavior to come, and there is a single bird standing behind the rest holding a sand eel in its bill, as if unsure of whom to offer it to. As I walk toward the island, I can see a big flock on the tidal sands beyond it. They rise up crying, then settle down again, but there are no birds to be seen on the nesting site.

The next day a shore wind is blowing and moving patches of fog across the salt marsh. More terns are racing in and out, appearing and reappearing through the fog. They swing back and forth on the downwind. With their graceful tails fanning out and drawing in, they twist and dive into the waters of the creek. "Keearrh!" they cry, and "Kip-kip!" as they slant off across the ditched, potholed marsh and its coarse grasses. There is an uplifting to their bodies. Their flight tests all the buffeting, seaside air, and the shores ring with a new mode of attachment.

The arrival of terns is gradual, cumulative. Although they roost at low tide on nearby peat ledges and tidal flats, or dive for fish, they fail to occupy the nesting site for some days. After arriving offshore, a flock may occasionally fly over the territory and small numbers will land temporarily, but it takes a while before any of them spend much time there during daylight hours, and it is longer still before they stay there at night. In other regions along the coastline, large flocks, possibly late, excited, and making up for lost time, may land on an offshore island all at once, coming in from high up, then dropping down and dashing back and forth like a snow squall before alighting.

A general arrival of terns along the coastline can be sudden and highly dramatic. At staging areas such as the shallow, saltwater bay inside Monomoy, the sandy spit extending south from the southern tip of Cape Cod, the skies will be empty of them one day and filled with their beautiful advent the next. Populations gather and separate here; the majority of terns, perhaps 20,000, moving north to the Gulf of Saint Lawrence, and the rest settling along the Atlantic shore.

Local breeders skirt the land and then begin to gather in small groups off the peripheries of their prospective nesting territories, which it takes them some days to occupy. Any flock seems to need an accumulative crowd momentum to encourage individuals to settle in.

Terns share an inherent nervousness about the predatory lands they come to. Their motions are typically precise and graceful, but their overall behavior has a nerve-sprung, touch-and-go feel to it. Their elastic bonding with the territory comes out in their motions of flying toward it, flying away. Then as their numbers increase, they begin to draw closer. I have seen something like this in schooling fish, an organic throw that aims for the center it is attracted to, circling, trying out, drawing in until it succeeds.

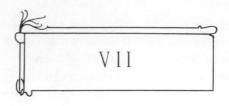

VII

The Rhythm of the Year

When I first saw the alewives pressing in to spawn, my own unexpressed emotions were almost as intense as those of the children screaming on the banks of the brook. These fish were silent messengers of a planetary depth that makes us cry out, or go on voyages. It could not be said that they were only repeating what they had done before. They were the personified power of a sea whose journeys are endless. The terns too, who might be said to have more direct parallels to our own visual equipment and conscious awareness than a fish, bring in undiscovered space. I am continually grateful to these migrants for coming in to assure me that where I am is on their map. Nothing thrives in exile.

As a nonscientist, I am about as far from reaching scientific conclusions as I am from a final knowledge of the birds themselves. But it is the open-ended experience of a common earth that moves my curiosity. The birds help me to reach. That is why I have been going out at night during this season of arrival, as the clouds cross each

≈

other in their flying passage and the stars shine out between the lifted arms of the trees. I think of the terns as they beat their way north. I imagine them flying over blue and green ocean waters, skirting storms, bending to the wind, dropping from side to side with their long wings, hovering and diving, until they home in on territories they have kept in their memory.

So far as long-distance travelers are concerned, each kind has its own far off feeding as well as breeding ranges. The timing and direction of migration differs in each one, or they do not migrate at all, like the sexually immature terns that stay where they are. The Kerguelen tern of the Indian Ocean, for example, stays close to the remote islands where it breeds.

One thinks of fluidity, migratory waves, and wide dispersals in connection with some birds such as petrels, which spread out during migration. Others, like the terns, are more closely knit, whether in small groups or fairly large flocks; but they all return consistently to their territories and have to be credited with a remarkable sense of direction.

The question of how birds navigate has occupied investigators for a long time. The average bystander might be justified in wondering whether the advanced machines and instruments our world uses to move from one end of the globe to the other with such speed and accuracy might not hinder us from understanding how the birds do it. While one world overcomes the elements, the other incorporates them. There is at least a considerable gap in our understanding of what the birds are able to accomplish, and what they are, which is a partly invisible quantity. Still, neither of us can abandon the sun and the stars.

The ancient Polynesians were able to make round trips of thousands of miles over the open ocean with little but the fixed stars to guide them, and it has long been suspected that birds might employ them too. Restless spring warblers about to migrate from Europe were put in a planetarium with the same star patterns that the birds could normally see on a clear night. The birds then faced in the direction of the migratory path they would take at this time of the year. When these patterns were shifted to another part of the planetarium sky, the birds changed the angle of their position accordingly.

Recognizable stars, in other words, can help the birds to align themselves on their normal flight path. Scientists have investigated other clues as well, such as a solar compass. It was found that birds used the sun as a reference point in maintaining their heading. Experiments have shown that they are also sensitive to the earth's magnetic field as a compass. The earth itself is a great magnet from which magnetic fields of force extend, varying in intensity from one pole to the other. They can be shown on a map as wavy contours girdling the globe from east to west. Birds heading in a polar direction are apparently able to keep on course by sensing these variants as they go, especially on dark and cloudy nights when the stars are obscured.

Traveling over the sea, terns may be able to locate themselves through low frequency, or "infra sounds," inaudible to us, such as the distant sound of the surf. They may also be able to hear storms at a distance, or the wind off inland hills and mountains. And it is not hard to understand how birds with their keen vision are able to recognize landmarks and consistent patterns in the seas over which they fly.

Prevailing winds play a vital part in aiding and directing these migrations. Typically, the migration of small land birds during the autumn waits on a northwest wind, with rapidly falling temperatures. Those heading nonstop from Canada and New England to the Caribbean islands, or further on to the north coast of South America, fly out to sea, after having waited for some days inshore for the right conditions. Flocks moving in a southerly direction fly from 2,000 to 3,000 kilometers to reach their destination, a journey of from three to four days. Others heading too far to the east encounter trade winds south of Bermuda which help to keep them on a consistent course.

One blustery September day, on the coast of Nova Scotia, I stood on a bold, grassy headland facing the Atlantic. On the brow of the hill was a wood of thickets and low trees where many restless land

~

birds were gathering, flitting between the openings. The headland
was a jumping off place where they waited for the passage of a strong
cold front, not venturing out from the woodland during the day, for
fear of predators.

Back of the coastline, not far away, was a sheltered inlet, with a
marsh and a beach. At low tide, hundreds of shorebirds were feeding
over the beach, pecking away at the sands. Just offshore was a thick
bed of glistening, slick brown kelp, its fronds and long stems heav-
ing and nodding in the shallow tidal waters. A few of the smaller
birds scurried over it, hunting for crustaceans. Suddenly, a sharp-
skinned hawk, dark in the afternoon light, stooped in low from off
the hillside behind the shore. It plucked a sandpiper from the bed
of kelp, hitting it with one foot, simultaneously carrying it off in its
talons as it flew toward a line of trees in the background.

No one will miss the sandpiper, lost among countless other casu-
alties. Not even the other shorebirds, which had cleared out fast as
the hawk attacked, could have missed it. In their quick fear, they
had swung off like a wave and disappeared. The death of one is the
death of multitudes, but by the light of the sea, each single identity
was as brilliant as it was evanescent.

The scale of these world migrations is staggering. They answer to
the body of the earth, and to planetary law. The long-distance migrants
fly far overhead, unseen, unless an exhausted bird drops down on
the boat we are traveling in. We who speed back and forth on asphalt
tracks are seldom aware of them. Yet there they go, in their great
reality, flying for thousands of miles at such high altitudes that they
are almost deprived of oxygen. They travel for days and nights, through
sunlight and starlight, buffeted by the winds. Hundreds run out of
energy, fall out, and die. They speed ahead, little birds—which many
people dismiss as being a minor, if colorful, part of nature—on a
high plane of sacrifice and commitment. To praise them is to distinguish ourselves. We are both allied to tidal fires that move us out on
destinations not man but earth intended.

It has been suspected for a long time that there must be some
internal reason for the fact that birds know when to leave their win-

tering areas and head north, or conversely, persuade them south again. It is certainly clear, in the temperate zone, that seasonal changes affect an animal's biology as they do the plants, while regardless of the reasons for it, spring uplifts the human spirit. The increase in daylight that begins in January in our latitude, followed by a gradual rise in temperature, begins to make the world of life move up and out. So the skunk cabbage spears up from semi-frozen marsh mud, and later on the white starflower blooms on the woodland floor. The alewives start to come in when seasonal changes in coastal waters, of light and temperature, stimulate their reproductive system. Why, on the other hand, should a species like the tern move north out of wintering grounds in equatorial regions where the length of days remains the same? There is now some evidence that the metabolic changes that start the terns on their way must occur irrespective of local conditions.

Unless you imagine that the world sea is all one to the seabirds and that they might know any of its ancestral directions instinctively, it seems astonishing that some long-distance migrants are able to cross a trackless ocean which they have never traveled before, to reach a coast they have never seen. But such is the case with sooty terns in the first year of life. Fledged in the Dry Tortugas off southern Florida, they migrate all the way across the tropical Atlantic to the Gulf of Guinea in Africa. Only the young seem to make such a migration. The adults also leave their breeding grounds after the season is over, but appear to go no farther than the neighboring Gulf of Mexico and the Caribbean. The route these juveniles take is apparently 20 percent longer than a direct line traced across the Atlantic would take them. The reason is that the longer route presents them with less resistance from storms and prevailing winds.

W. B. Robertson had this to say to those who can trace the terns either in their mind's eye or on a map:

> The migrants cross the tropical cyclone belt of the Atlantic by the southerly lag of the route in the western Caribbean and make their easting in the nearly storm-free area of the extreme southern Carib-

bean. Hurricanes are the chief known cause of the death of fledged sooty terns, and intersecting storms in August and September, 1901–1967, were twice as frequent (154 compared with 78) along the direct route compared with the route we believe the terns follow. A southeasterly track along the Guyanan coast carries migrants across the northeast trade wind belt and enables them to complete their Atlantic crossing in the light winds and calms of the intertropical convergences. Approaching Africa on this course should at times encounter favorable winds of the onshore monsoon. Because most of the flight is opposite to the prevailing directions of surface winds and storm movement, a route that voids or minimizes the hazards of more frequent hurricanes and stronger contrary winds may be particularly significant for survival. Prevailing winds doubtless assist their return flight, the most favorable conditions probably occurring in February and March when the northeast trade winds extend farthest south.*

As creatures of the atmosphere, birds are highly sensitive to subtleties and changes in the wind. Their navigational abilities imply an awareness of wind and water currents that keep them on course. The migration of birds has followed wilderness lanes and flyways over all parts of the globe and many migrants seem to have an inbred memory of them. This may lie dormant in them for years, even after they have been semi-domesticated, like certain wild swans and geese. For colonial birds that travel in flocks, the ability to set off again on ancestral flyways may be in part a matter of racial memory and in part a learned skill, transmitted from one generation to the next.

Scientists have concluded that the right timing required to set a bird off on its migratory journey is based on an "endogenous (growing from within) rhythm" which acts like a biological clock, similar to what is found in a great many other animals, including ourselves. Annual rhythms in the birds are equated both with the seasons and the solar year. That migrants like young sooty terns should be able to head off for Africa on their own for the first time may be accounted

*W. B. Robertson, "Transatlantic Migration of Juvenile Sooty Terns," *Nature* 223, no. 66182 (May 1969): 632–634.

for through genetic inheritance and the subtle flow of hormones. As much to the point perhaps is that deep within them lie the rhythms of an earth which has always been their guide and mysterious home.

At the same time, they can learn from experience. Young and inexperienced birds may depend on an inner rhythm to send them on their way and in the right direction, but birds that have made the migration before know how to keep on course more accurately. When displaced, they can correct themselves and find their right heading again. Experiment seems to have proved that their internal state not only keeps them on course but determines the length of their journey and its destination. However automatic this may sound, there is no reason to believe that they are unable to adjust their movements to new conditions, such as a lack of food or stormy weather, along the way.

The complexities of global migration are not solved by the theory of the endogenous rhythm. They belong to more profound affinities with the earth than we are yet aware of. The mysteries are still ahead. I am a tern, in attributes of sight and feeling, in fear and anger, the passion to exist. Still, its startling and unique qualities, as a member of the kingdom of the air, is at a lasting distance from me. What it knows that man does not ought to be an inspiration to us all.

Charles Walcott, who has carried out intensive studies for many years of the homing ability in pigeons, has this to say in a recent article:

> We have learned that the pigeon senses a world quite different from ours—a world of pressure changes, infrasonic sounds, polarized light, subtle vibrations, naturally fluctuating magnetic fields, and perhaps other cues yet to be discovered. Given the limitations of our own sensory world and our bond to earth's surface, solving the mystery of how pigeons find their way is indeed a challenging and intriguing goal. The humble homing pigeon, in a way, is a window enabling us to look out at a mysterious world.*

Natural History (November 1989).

The domesticated, city pigeon is descended from the rock dove that nested on cliffsides in Europe. It would seem as if this was a relatively sedentary bird, though with a powerful sense of its home territory. Modern racing pigeons have been released a thousand miles from their home loft and have returned to it. What more might those global travelers, the terns, be guided by, exposed as they are to the vast distances and varying conditions of the seas?

The terns, this spring, are still flying in and accumulating on their territories, establishing nesting sites with agitation and ceremony. They seem to me like explorers from a great outer world from which we have been excluding ourselves. The closest I can come to it is by going down to the shore again, where I am exposed to stripped down, elemental demands. The terns, however, identify it with their lives. Sand dunes, beaches, or islands become new centers for wild collusion and energy. They are not homes, or safe havens, so much as mediums for life's desire, persisting through immortal danger.

Walking across the marsh, or down to the beach, in order to watch terns has meant that I have had to observe them from a distance, and during daylight hours. It was not until Helen Hays, director of the Great Gull Island Program, invited me out there that I was able to spend days and nights in their midst. The island, only seventeen acres in extent, lies out at the mouth of Long Island Sound, and is reached by boat from the Connecticut shore. It has been maintained as a research center for terns by the American Museum of Natural History since 1965. The army constructed a massive coast artillery fort there to protect the entrance of New York harbor, beginning with the Spanish-American war, from enemies who never put in an appearance. It was abandoned after World War II and its structures dynamited, or left to be reduced by the weather. Terns, which were known to have nested on the island before the fort was built, began to come in to nest some ten years later. By the early 1970s, there were altogether about 7,000 common and roseate terns nesting on the island, or 3,500 pairs, numbers which have greatly increased since that time, owing to devoted and diligent management. The roseates, as in other parts of the world, have been in the minority.

In 1988, there were 6,000 nesting pairs of commons, and 1,200 of roseates.

It was in the month of May that I first saw Great Gull Island. The boat approached it toward sundown, over molten-copper waters. The buildings of the old fort almost completely covered the little island, with what remained of its concrete walls, bunkers, and towers hunkered down between grassy shoulders. To stabilize the shoreline, the army had covered it with huge boulders, or traprock. As the island became distinguishable, the terns showed up as white, scattered chips sailing through the air, and as we came closer still, their gargling, harsh cries sounded through a strong wind and the lapping of the waves.

The first night was wide out with its sea air and the stars. With empty windows, abandoned streets, and installations, the ruined fort was like an American Pompeii, and I could hear terns whenever I woke up during the night. There were scattered cries from the near end of the island, and now and then an abrupt "Kraak!" or "Keeat" from a roseate would sound overhead, with the timbre of a comb plucked by the fingers, as single birds or pairs swept past the walls or over the roofs. They were resonant, imperious cries across a night massed with starry directions.

The birds, as I heard them leading and pursuing each other, called me out under the star-pitted sky. I left my sleeping bag, walked out into the empty street, and was made dizzy by the vast heights beyond me, heights that could direct a bird on migration . . . a tern for a star. Surely, I thought, they can be guided by the constellations on a clear night, whatever else could help them to define and correct their course, they knew the stars better than I. This ancestral race embodied the reaches of the world. What could it be but strict in its motions, intense in its performance, with such exalted standards to follow?

I heard "Keearr" now as a major tribal cry, and I put it off against our scattered mechanical thunder and human spreading along the inland shore. If we based our civilization wholly on the premise that

we could neutralize or disguise the high risk all nature requires of
its lives, were we really protecting ourselves?

I thought of the intensely crowded city not far away, millions of
us preoccupied with maintaining order and communication. Biological analogies had been made before between human colonies and
those of ants or seabirds. We were all part of a planetary tension and
tumult. On the other hand, I thought of the human race with its
superior brains, in an unsettled world, shifting between applied reason and violently misapplied emotion, as having connections with
its natal earth that were decidedly uneasy. Can this ship of civilization, orbiting in its own space, be controlled by conscious effort, or
is there another passion in us that has no outcome to reveal? The
universe hatches great desires, both intricate and cruel.

On Gull Island, the terns were making scrapes for their nests on
gravelly ground, on bare stretches where the fort's concrete was
exfoliating, and along stony parts of the beach. The roseates nested
deep between the crevices of the traprock. When the research staff
and their weekend helpers made daily nest checks there, they had to
contort their backs and necks to capacity. Instead of being on the
fringe of a salt marsh, this island was far out on the water, swept
around by tidal rips and currents, within the sound of fog horns,
whipping winds and water breaking against its rocky shores. Planes
droned overhead while oil tankers moved by over the waters of the
sound. While sea music kept booming through glistening light, I
watched a group of terns as they stood facing into a twenty- to thirty-
mile-an-hour wind, streamlined, stiff as weathervanes, hunkered down,
their heads and necks pulled in. Occasionally the wind would throw
them off balance; their tail ends teetered up and they had to readjust
themselves, with a fussy tucking and retucking of their wings. The
pure black on the crowns of their heads curved down to the nape of
their necks, cloths of distinction. Occasionally, one of them would
fly up and hang on the force of the air for a while.

On this home ground, they seemed even more intimately con-
nected with the roll of the seas, lifting and wind-conducted across

the wrinkled waters, roving away. Weather of all kinds was their medium. I had seen them now, here and on the Cape, flying in out of the fog, in lightning and hail, flying up against a rippling, fiery sea at sundown. All their swooping and chasing, swerving and gliding, was rhythmically allied with the shallow seas along the coast and the open coast where they followed their transverse migratory routes.

I thought of seabirds profoundly oriented to the dark, gray-green distances over which they traveled, having a sense in them of global reach. The way the planet heeled was in their flight, the way it raced in the universe. The world to a tern is not consciously mapped and continually corrected, but one which had been followed and known in them long before "discovery." As well as the fixed stars, they had followed the moving landscape of the earth, the coastal run of islands and bays, the oceanic currents and storms, the continental lakes and marshes, feeling the atmosphere as they migrated over the millennia. It was the intruder like myself who could see the world as a whole and at the same time have it slip away from him, an intruder who had partly lost this ability to find his way.

We speed ahead, though with a remarkable lack of inner confidence. We make much of the change we are responsible for, but scarcely know where it is taking us. It is as if, on this global home, our power to possess was more formidable than any of our mental trajectories into empty space. Ignorant of what moves us, we claim the planet for ourselves. I saw how the terns, more precise about their chosen ground, ready in their perfect wings to meet variety, coming on again to fish and breed in the context of an ever changing earth, were, in a sense, on these islands ahead of us, staking out equally legitimate claims. We needed their wisdom. To dispossess them in too many places would be to destroy a genius in essentials.

VIII

Ritual

The month of May streams forward, in all its sequences of light. The air warms up, while southerly winds still battle with the north. In this transmigratory period, it still seems miraculous to me not that these seabirds can find their way, but that they possess such a sureness of place, from one pole to the other. It is a magic of fitness, of appropriate measure on a global scale, which they carry in their minds.

In terms of their behavior, terns are so spontaneous as to be inseparable from the present. At the same time, they exist in an eternal present insofar as they follow the dictates of the sun and the earth's travels around it. In a highly seasonal part of the world, we divide the year into spring, summer, autumn, and winter, but ultimately only one season dictates the infinitely varied terms of life to all creation. The clouds are only temporarily described by our classification of them into cirrus, nimbus, stratus, cumulus, and their variations. They take their forms from continuous motion, and those beings who follow that motion in themselves can never be on a lower scale than ourselves, who see fit to determine all stages of it in terms of material possession and the human mind. As played out in the birds, the planetary rhythms have a supremacy which cannot be violated or reduced. The terns arrive on their territories, as they will leave them, obeying certain time-honored rituals, which amount to a high form of courtesy which we might do well to respect.

The terns are in a state of great urgency as they gather offshore and begin to move in, aggravated in their need to pair up and nest. In the vicinity of the nesting site at Gray's Beach, a female is making constant, chittering cries as she waits on a sandbar for attention. A male hovers over a tidepool nearby, then twists in the air and makes a slanting dive into the surface to pick up a minnow, which he brings to her. The fish is accepted and swallowed, but she goes on begging, and he tries it twice again while I watch, to finally break off and leave her there, perhaps to be more satisfied by him, or another possible mate, later on. These early indecisions are common enough in courtship, but they might contain some underlying doubt as to whether or not the birds have come to the right place.

Gulls circle and romp together in the springtime air, while others are scattered over the tidal flats, musically calling. A man and his girl friend go idling and bumping each other down the beach, swaying like trees in a wind. I walk out over the complex map of the tidelands, across their ripples and watery lanes and shallow pools. It is a silvery landscape and the sky is sending down light showers like so much sea spray.

Water spurts up from a hole made by a clam. As the tide begins to move in, wavelets bob and duck around me, gradually covering and wreathing the sands. Through my field glasses, I see a pair of common terns strutting around each other, heads and necks stretched up, tails cocked, wings lowered and held out partly on their sides.

Further out over the sands is a pair of roseate terns, recognizable through their black bills, their longer tails, and feathers of a more uniformly light gray than the commons. They get their name from a pinkish flush on their breasts, not always visible except when the light strikes them at the right angle. The stance of these birds when courting is extremely elegant. Their tails project behind them like spars on a sailing vessel. Their velvety gray wings spread out like a cloak, the hem nearly touching the ground, and their shining black heads and beaks point cleanly toward the sky, in a pose that is highly strict and formalized.

On both sides of the Atlantic, the population of roseates has seriously declined. In America, they have been classified as an endangered species. The common terns, more aggressive and adaptable, have managed to hold their own for the time being, but not without help from individuals and institutions protecting their nesting sites. Roseates are more vulnerable to the twentieth century's worldwide disturbances, and are disappearing . . . a bird of classic style that ought to be as precious to us as the Parthenon has been to the Greeks. But we let the great architecture of life slip away from us and what we no longer see before us we are unable, or unwilling, to compare with the lesser standards by which we value the earth.

Many of the birds engaging in courtship behavior before they settle in to nest may have been premated, which is to say, paired up during the previous season. Either they have spent the winter together, or they have recognized each other on arriving in the vicinity of the site. Even though premated pairs will start in to court and nest without much delay, just as many seem to join the majority in days of ground and aerial display. This is a process through which pairs are finally "bonded," and the whole colony established. It is difficult at first to tell the difference between males and females, until pairs start to copulate before nesting. In these early days, three, four, or five birds displaying together is quite common, which makes distinguishing between the sexes even harder.

(I do not know of any ready shortcut to identifying males and females. Years ago, the warden of a colony of Sandwich and common terns in Great Britain told me that he could tell the difference by their voices. Since he had been listening to them all his life, as had his father before him, I had no reason to doubt him. He also contended that he could tell male from female by the way the black cap ended at the nape of the neck; it comes to more of a point in the male, and is a little squared off or blunted in the female. So far, at least, this last distinction has not worked for me, since the shape of the black feathers on their necks seems to depend on the way they happen to be holding their heads, up or down.)

J. M. Cullen, in her thesis on the Arctic terns,* describes an action she calls tilting in the mating display of the Arctics; the behavior of the commons is almost identical. These and other species have fully developed black caps during the breeding season, but their fall molt leaves them with a streaked or grayish patch on their heads, and a whitish forehead. The conclusion is that the black cap has a definite function during mating. In displaying before a potential mate, a bird will tilt its head so that the cap is hidden, or partly turned away from its partner. To show it directly seems to have an intimidating effect. If a female walks around a male in a "bent" position, with her beak pointed toward the ground—as opposed to an "erect" display with head and neck pointed upward—the male on his inside circle makes an effort to keep his cap turned away from her, because if she catches sight of it, she might move away.

Since males are probably made nervous, or put off, by the display of the cap as well, and since they are more aggressive than females in defense of territory, the display may have some significance as a threat, but is probably used more in avoidance and appeasement than as a direct challenge. If a male pecks at a female, or rushes toward her, she will tilt her cap to avoid further trouble, and males startled or frightened by something during a mating display, or while making their way through a neighbor's territory, will do the same.

Step by step, from the first hesitant approaches to the territory, to early nesting behavior, followed by established nests, egg laying, and the raising of chicks, the season is followed out with formality and underlying discipline. After the terns have begun to settle in, the sands are covered with little chain patterns made by their feet where

* "A Study of the Behavior of the Arctic Tern *(Sterna macrura),*" Thesis deposited at the Bodleian Library, Oxford, 1956.

they have strutted around each other, while a high and wide chasing, fluttering up, circling, and gliding goes on overhead, at times loose, easy, and pliable, and at others very fast. All this effort leads up to a means whereby a colony can occupy old nests, or establish new ones over a given space, with order and understood boundaries. (On some islands, pairs of terns have been seen coming back to their exact same nesting sites over a period of many years.) In general, a male attempts to lead a female down to a proposed site, often with several males chasing after him, especially if he is carrying a fish. The sorting out takes days on end; it amounts to a continual trying out, a continual falling short, or erosion, of the efforts of males and females to form their "pair bonds."

Males may even put a great deal of effort into trying to attract birds that may not be the right sex in the first place, such as a male who seems to be behaving momentarily like a female, or a female that is already mated. Sex recognition often takes time. The combination of attack and escape that is part of all their efforts to mate is also a factor in temporarily holding them back from the serious business of nesting. They are edgy. They engage in maneuvers which are broken off, time and again. But sooner or later, a female becomes satisfied that her suitor has chosen the right space of chosen ground to nest in.

(Much of the time spent in finding an appropriate mate probably has an element of critical judgment in it, so far as the female is concerned. She needs a mate who is going to bring in plenty of fish and choose a good nesting hollow in the first place, and that implies discrimination.)

Scraping out little hollows in the sand represents an early stage in courtship ritual, but it is a practice that serves to strengthen emotional ties. (Emotion plays a very strong part in the life of these birds.) After a male and female greet each other, posturing, the male may walk over to a preexisting hollow which he has chosen, then lower his breast while scratching out backward in the sand. If the female is interested enough, she may go over and stand by him, or even replace her suitor to enlarge the scrape on her own. Such scrapes are often called false by the ornithologists because they do not lead to a final nest.

In a similar way, the presentation of fish on the ground is another ceremonial act that strengthens their feelings toward each other. A male parading with a fish before a prospective mate does a sort of goose step, breast forward, in a very conscious way. It is an athlete or a soldier strutting his stuff, displaying his medals or his victorious presence before the girls. She begs for this precious gift, bent down in a submissive posture, while making eager, chittering cries like a chick being fed by its parent. At times she takes the fish, swallows it, and then flies away without any obvious sign of gratitude. Or a tension between them results in a tug-of-war. She snatches at the fish, and he holds on so that they are left with two halves.

In another version of this behavior, the female grabs at the fish and the male flies away with it, as if displeased. They share contradictory feelings at this stage of the game. She has a compulsion to lay eggs, and he to start in on the nest. This results in slight acts of aggression. The inner testing that marks their attempts to pair up implies that the male may be just as frightened as the female, or enough afraid of her so as not to surrender the fish.

As I watch them, distant as they are from my own sense of reality, I sense something of my own ambivalence. Seasons of hesitation, nerves sprung in the wind, characterize us both. On a deeper level, all this avian maneuvering with its wayward rhythms follows an uncompromising need that brings energy into our own affairs and fear to our hearts.

As the days go by, the activity becomes more intense. At least a few terns are displaying whenever I walk out over the marsh to watch them, at a viewing distance. One of a pair might be on the ground with wings cloaked and tail cocked, while the other circles over it. Three will land simultaneously. With necks craned in the same direction and wings held out, they look like uniformed soldiers on dress parade. Swift chases are going on in the air, involving three, or as many as five or six at a time. They are constantly engaged in flying up from the sandy hollows and hummocks, leading away, breaking off, settling down again, and day by day, the general clamor increases.

In their wild, formal, and repeated exercises, they also interchange with the sandy land they came to. Their rituals are rhythmically allied with the growing grasses now shaking and whipping in the wind, and with the waters trickling back and forth over the tidal flats, shivering, parting, coming together again under silken clouds.

Courtship flights follow the two main types of ground display, combining elements of both. A male with beak pointed downward, as in the bent display, tries to lead a female who adopts the erect posture, or a less extreme equivalent of it, with head and neck extended and tilted upward. They fly past each other, each one alternately falling behind and overtaking the other so that it looks as if they were swinging in the air.

When a male carries a fish on these flights, as a superior form of attraction, it often starts with three or more birds engaging in much evasive action, eventually evolving into two. The remaining pair then fly off together, interchanging positions as they go. The bird in front may swing downward and to the side, while the other flies over and past it. Then the procedure is reversed as the bird now in the lead moves back and downward. There is a lovely, tilting balance to their flight. The male sounds a clear "Keera," while the female may cry "Kip-kip" or "Tik-tik," and then his call may change to a rasping "Koh-koh-keearrh."

So the sorting out in the colony goes on and on, and I hear many other cries as the birds go through their nearly incessant flying up and landing again, many stridently challenging, connective cries. Isn't this urgent practice, for days on end, what we are continually required to do, at times veering off wildly in the wrong direction?

The tension in these flights, the resolution of conflict in these rituals, is in the spring itself, where the ruffed grouse drums and the gulls bow to each other. No life lacks ceremony.

The tension of opposites lies behind the perfection of form and all appearances. So a leaf stirs in the wind and lifts like a bird; the insect is the image of the leaf it inhabits; the shiny seed of a red maple has a cracked back like a winged beetle. Unlikeness seeks out likeness everywhere. Throughout these relationships, unendingly renewed, are the elements of evasion and affinity, touch and recoil. The hunger generated in the worlds of life, the fish to rise and be met by a predatory bird, the fish to suspend or procreate in the tension of the waters, is back of all memory and behavior.

The more I see of courtship flights, the more they compare with human games. The natural ease of great ball players is in them, of champion skaters, or ballet dancers. At the same time, I doubt whether there is much that can equal their high flight and its glide to earth. This culminating flight involves the circling upward of a pair to a high altitude, with one bird leading the other. At some point, one of them folds its wings slightly and starts to glide easily toward the ground, while the other follows. The two of them bank back and forth from one side to the other, swaying and side-slipping together as if their whole life had been a training for such an act.

The roseates, a cut in elegance above the commons, have a beautifully reaching look to their bodies as they glide together. When a pair flies slowly over the territory, their wings, stroking with an effortless assurance that accompanies the steady flow of a wave, appear to lean and hang on the air. Pairs of both species will circle high over a colony, but the roseates often fly out in a great circling fetch over the sea. I have watched a pair of roseates rising so high in the brilliantly blue sky that I have almost lost sight of them, but their impeccable snowy feathers shone in the light of the sun, while their catamaran-like tails showed as white filaments. (Their tails are longer and more flexible than the commons, floating and bouncing on the wind.) Their skill is dazzling. In a strong wind, they look as if they were flying backward as they ascend, but they are in perfect control. With both commons and roseates, a very fast chasing and circling upward will often end in a wide zigzagging glide down.

Roseates arrive on the nesting grounds later than the commons, although their spring migration is probably faster, since they are

superior flyers. While common terns move up the coastline, relatively close to shore, roseates fly higher and farther out over the
ocean. By early to mid-June, after most of the commons are incubating eggs, or brooding chicks, some roseates will still be engaged
in courtship flights. Nothing exceeds their slip-streaming across the
sky, incomparably lithe and limber. At times they skate through the
sky as if shot from a sling, and at others they sail like kites on a high
wind, or knife through the air like mackerel in undulant waters.
They remind me then of William Blake's "arrows of desire."

Both species make spectacular glides. After a passage of synchronized swinging, they appear to start tumbling, or revolving high in
the air. This is apparently due to a form of gliding in which they
turn as they fall, tilting one wing above the other on a vertical instead
of horizontal plane. Whereas common terns may start a downward
glide from five or six hundred feet, and Roseates from still higher,
Sandwich Terns will circle up to several thousand feet. I have been
told that from that great height, a pair will drop at a speed of sixty
to seventy miles an hour, the pressure on their outer primary feathers making a papery, drumming sound. They plunge down toward
the ternery at an angle of about sixty degrees until they are within
three to four hundred feet of the ground, then sheer upward, to
circle and land in an easy, finished way together. The whole arc of
this masterful performance may take in as much as two miles. What
a surpassing way to express the feelings of opposite sexes freed of
their restraint!

A friend of mine once said to me as I was rhapsodizing about this
dance of the birds: "How does that relate to me? Tell us about
ourselves." Hadn't I suggested parallels enough? I realize that very
few of us, even when we are in love, have the ability to launch into
paired maneuvers a thousand feet in the air. But I suspect that what
stopped him from making the connection was the idea of "nature,"
which he had long since left to the scientists and the sentimentalists.

Courtship in animals follows certain stereotyped patterns that go
back so far in the vast flow of evolution that we can only guess as to
their origins. In that sense alone there is no use oversimplifying these

rituals in our favor. Accustomed to pigeons billing and cooing in the city, people are inclined to think of birds as helplessly repetitive, incapable of reflecting on their own actions. Year after year, I have heard it said of the alewives, they just come back and do the same thing. Yet these fish, on their annual journey, are once again engaged in a revolutionary mission. To put down the birds in their sexual flights and courtship rituals is to underrate the profundity of the rhythm of the year. It also passes over their closeness to earth environments whose every mood may be a matter of life and death.

In the existence of a tern, love as we know it may be only an incident, which if at all relevant, seems to a high degree made up of aggravation. Yet in a short season, they carry out the paramount needs of love, and we ought not to be no niggardly or self-limiting as to deny it to them. The same, imperative inner demands send us ahead on our own migrations. Subconscious motivation is a common property of life. We are unable to escape our origins.

The inner conflict between nesting pairs and its resolution comes out of an earth engagement as mysterious as anything we will ever know. The term "pair bond" seems excessively limited by comparison.

Wild chases, accompanied by a great deal of clamor, increase as more birds come in and the colony establishes itself. The friction between attraction and intimidation fires their energies. At times, the element of hostility which is a part of their flights gives way to a fight, usually short-lived. A pair may start off easily enough but then drop to the ground with angry, gargling cries, in a flurry of beating wings. Or two birds, wings rapidly stroking, will rise from the territory, partly turning around each other and moving backward at the same time. The one rises above the other, and they will keep alternating in this way, each trying to be the one on top. It is an action that has some of the characteristics of a fight between two males on the ground, but often turns into a paired flight that looks like courtship. These "flutter-ups" are mainly associated with nesting territory, and play some part in the recognition by individual birds of their separate claims—which leads to the idea that they are engaged in by males.

A vigorous fight starts up between two male roseates on the ground. They peck violently at each other, wings beating, but quickly break off. It might be said that the fight has served to define a mutual tolerance, an understanding that can be translated into a few inches of territory.

Roseates, as compared with the commons, which like more open ground, choose fairly thick vegetation to nest in, often making small, tunnellike openings at the edge of a heavy growth of grass. In some areas, they also nest under boulders or in rock burrows where they are narrowly confined, and where mating rituals have to be performed in a highly stylized manner. The male goes in first, followed by the female. She starts by facing him, then pivots around, posturing, while he lowers his head, calling "Uh-uh-uh-uh." Then the female goes back out, while he engages in some scraping motions. Terns know where their boundaries are, though they may be invisible to us, especially out in the open, but rock walls enforce proximity, and the ritual has to be precisely carried out, or the pair will fight.

On open ground, a pair of roseates weave around each other in tight little circles, like matadors with their capes, while bowing and craning their glossy black heads, tail feathers held up behind their silvery backs, wings bowed out at their sides. There is something stiff and military about it. This is a ritual which is perfectly tuned to the rhythms of space and cannot be transgressed. Its formality does not allow the slightest deviation, being no more tyrannical, no less pure than those ice crystals I see forming on the water's surface as winter comes. We invent our instruments, each one an improvement on the last in our efforts to surpass the bonds of nature, but life's perfected instruments are bound to laws beyond our ability to see.

A male common tern flies in with a fish and offers it to his prospective mate, having tried it before without success. At last, the right signal has been received. She takes the fish and eats it, and he is stimulated to copulate with her. He circles her, four or five times over, while she turns, only slightly, after which he mounts her, standing high on her back for a minute, then quickly lowering to copulate. Then he postures briefly and they both fly off.

During the action another bird stands nearby, posturing in a sort of half-hearted way, as if it entertained the notion of joining them. For terns, three is not always a crowd. I have heard of a case in which an unmated male joined a pair that was already engaged in incubating eggs and was allowed to help. It sounds as if the married couple just got accustomed to having him around and gave him a key to the home, but there is a less whimsical explanation for it. Among various kinds of breeding birds there are unmated individuals, not sexually engaged with the nesting parents, who may help with incubating eggs, or even with the feeding and rearing of the young. Such helpers are often younger birds who are in a sense shut out. They have difficulty in colonies where space is zealously guarded and occupied. As independents, they are not able to find a place to breed or obtain a mate.

Efforts at copulation do not always succeed right away. A male may mount a female and stand on her back for minutes at a time, teetering a little in an absent-minded way before he climbs off, with nothing accomplished. Repeated efforts are often made, but with consummation, egg laying soon follows.

In another part of the colony, a bird slightly enlarges a scrape in the sand, digging out backward while his mate stands aside. Then he stands back while she moves in to the nest, plucking lightly at some grass. Finally both posture, circling each other, and then stand together on the nest facing into the wind, with an air of proud attachment.

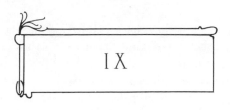

Outflights

Terns have always had to adjust to the dangers of the land. It shows in their tenacity as well as in their frequent displays of alarm. They survive on a shifting balance between success and disaster. The territories they occupy were never consistently hospitable. Adversity comes in waves over endless periods of time and since terns are often wave-like in their responses, they have always maintained a fierce and bending adjustment to it. Yet in this century of man, they have been increasingly forced out of more favorable sites by the enormous pressure of men and gulls.

In their behavior, halfway between risk and necessity, there is always an underlying tension. On our human level, this is familiar enough. The struggle to reconcile order with inherent disorder is constant, with any individual, family, or community. Everyone experiences our unending efforts to put reason in the same world with emotions that threaten anarchy. We may not think of these conflicts as applying to birds, whose choices seem far more narrow, but I see these embattled terns as playing a similar game. They are full of a tense reconciliation of opposites in everything they do, resolved in terms of innate skill and restraint, applied to a harried destiny. From this there can be no divergence.

The whole structure of their society is an art in itself, fitting the simple to the complex. Tern behavior, in no passive sense, accommodates the highly changing world they live in, with its constant element of chance. The daily erosion in their early attempts to pair up, their adherence to ritual, their constant posturing throughout the season, their nervous intensity, is less restrictive than a way to make it possible to shift territories, change mates, or find new sources of food. This life exercise is like a balance wheel defined by variance, exposed to all the tides.

By the last week in May, most pairs start nesting and incubating eggs. However, courtship behavior, at least in a flourishing colony, can be seen throughout the summer. There usually are a certain number of young, unmated birds and even occasional strays from other colonies, such as pairs that may have deserted their nests during the season and are now trying again. Shifting between nesting areas is rare with individuals, as distinct from the wholesale desertion of a colony, but it has been known to occur, at times from fairly distant points.

Their clamoring, their maneuvering, their minor acts of aggression, is incessant. They are alert to any opportunity that might arise. A male carrying a fish in his bill adds to his powers of attraction, but he has to watch his neighbors. A fish is irresistible to other birds who want it for their own displays or, later in the season, who are feeding their young. Any bird, male or female, with a fish in its bill can expect interference. A fish carrier is importuned, stolen from, tricked, and chased at any time in the season. Not only is life in a tern colony full of rhythmic exchanges that are a pleasure to watch, but common greed, the taking of unfair advantage, and an unavoidable tendency to be petulant are fundamental too.

As the colony becomes more established, it is still wildly busy with posturing, crying birds, flying out over the water and returning, while others sit quietly on their nests. The commons become much more aggressive toward intruders. If you come too close to the nesting area, a male, or several of them, is bound to come tearing out at high speed and dive at your head, with a wild "krrrrack!" that has such a rasping, saw-toothed edge to it that you feel as if this small bird means to rip you up from stem to stern.

"What are these terns really like?" It would be tempting to answer that they are nasty, aggressive little creatures always quarreling with their neighbors. But their behavior, however it may look from the outside, is always contained within the often beautiful means by which they attain their ends. Their restraint is as marked as their aggressiveness. Behind this nearly constant agitation, there exists an insistence on order. A tern's consciousness is so unlike ours as to belong to a foreign, and, we falsely assume, a limited sphere; but it is as dependent as we are on the dark tidal powers that drive the worlds of life, and lift them into the light.

Their nervous readiness to fly off, even when sitting on their eggs, is always apparent, as individuals, or when numbers spontaneously fly off together. Silent flights, as distinct from noisy ones at the approach of an intruder, are always latent in a tern colony, and often take place without apparent cause. Once I saw a small group on a beach fly out silently over the water and back again, though I saw nothing that could have alarmed them, unless it was the wave that sharply smacked the sands as they do at intervals on a changing tide. A man or a dog will jump at unexpected sounds, but with terns which act together it is not just a matter of being startled. These silent "outflights" of theirs have a certain eerie quality so that they have been given the term "dreads." "Panics" is another designation, or "alarms," though an alarm flight, if the distinction is correct, may be accompanied by an outcry.

A sudden noise, an unexpected movement, even the sight of a single bird flying quickly and abruptly out to sea may send up at least a part of a colony. For a second or two, the normal volume of their crying lies down; then, all at once, with the same spontaneous discipline as a flock of sanderlings, they wheel out over the water, with only the sound of their swishing wings to be heard.

A panic may occur when the sudden blast of a boat horn is heard from offshore, whereupon the entire colony sweeps up in silence, to wheel and swerve over the water, its members dashing and falling like autumn leaves. As one integrated flock, they dive low across the surface, rise into the wind, and return to their territory, though they may not settle down until after several of these wild forays. The tern warden in Britain told me that at times, high-frequency sounds going through the colony may cause a panic—even snapping your fingers can do it—and that such a panic can occur before the onset of a storm, because of their nervous sensitivity toward the weather. He made a distinction between major panics and "pockets" of them made by small groups occurring throughout the season.

A common element in these flights is that they take place over the water, the terns conspicuously avoiding the land, just as they do when they first arrive. Ornithologists assume that since water provides escape from predators, as the land does not, the bird's reaction is a sign of fear. They swoop low over the water at first, the way they do when a hawk flushes them out of their nests, and they also flock together more tightly than usual, which is characteristic of other birds, as well as other animals. Schooling fish also bunch together when they are being pursued or when suddenly alarmed.

Most silent flights, on the other hand, are not caused by predators at all. In fact, both commons and Arctics are so aggressive that they are more likely to mob a predator than fly away from it, though a great-horned owl in the night is probably an exception. It is also worth noting that continued outflights later in the season may coincide with prolonged disturbance, or an exceptional lack of food, and could signal an early departure from the colony.

These flights occur under so many different conditions, and often for such apparently contradictory reasons, that it is hard to assign them a function. They belong to the still indecipherable nature of a tern, and this gives them a special fascination.

Modes of response such as these might be given a specific meaning, given enough trained observation, but since they are part of the psyche of the animal, they are not easily pinned down. Silence as a condition communicates itself instantaneously between the terns, and it may be one of the means by which their basic unity is adhered to during the nesting season. These strangely silent, abrupt departures always seem to be less a matter of stated functions than a display of psychic energy, out of some electric quality of awareness.

Helen Hays, director of the Great Gull Island Program, once told me of having spent the night in a blind on the edge of the colony, with its thousands of terns. She kept dozing off and waking to the high-pitched, sporadic cries all around her. Suddenly, precipitously, at about five o'clock in the morning, the racket was succeeded by a total silence. All the terns had left at once, to fly out over the sea. It might have been one of their dread flights, or an outflight responding to the light of dawn. The sudden hush left her with a momentary feeling of desertion and dread in the spirit. The whole earth speaks within us in mysterious ways.

How can you put the clumsy human finger on the spontaneity in the worlds of life? The fish swerve away from me with the quickness of flowing water. Terns or sanderlings move like swift interpreters of a traveling air that none of the rest of us can catch. Their flights cannot be understood through references to the central nervous system alone. They carry an element of fear that possesses us as well, and goes beyond thought.

I walk out across the marsh, as I have done so many times in the past, while the earth around me extends its engagements in the tendrils of growth and receptiveness. The faint smell of fish comes to me on the warm wind. Peering in to the waters of the tidal inlet, I catch sight of a tiny, wiggling elver, materializing as if nothing like it had ever swum into my sight before. We know the migratory route of the common eel to its spawning grounds in the far distance of the Sargasso Sea, but there they die, and no one has ever seen them die. Their progeny carry this unknown quantity across the wide Atlantic, an inner space on oceanic terms.

A few terns are crying in the distance, but not in such shrill volume as in former years. The Gray's Beach colony has been dwindling. For the past five years, no young have been fledged at all, probably because of consistent predation. The area has been posted to discourage human intruders, but it is close enough to the mainland so that owls, foxes, and other predators have had easy access to it. Terns can endure such pressure up to a point, but then they move out if they have other sites to move to, but space is being foreclosed along these crowded shores.

We have created a world of disengagement where human society is as much affected as the terns. Our ties to the life of land and water have been frayed so that we too have been dispossessed. All of us are "way out," as an old Cape Codder once said of me when we met in town. We are compulsive migrants, following mechanical routes. Yet who is to escape the universe and its abiding signals carried in on the wind, lifted with the tides?

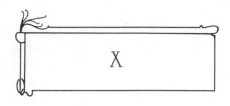

X

The Dispossessed

The fact that the terns seemed to be deserting Gray's Beach came as a shock to me. It was as if I thought I had found some permanent center in a local place without having to move. But that was not consistent with the way of the terns, whose whole life is a passionate response to motion and change. Without such rightful guides, we short-term landowners will never emerge on the other side of our own darkness. They who climb the sun have introduced me to the wider priorities of space.

The advancing season has covered the borders of the marsh channels and ditches with the new green of the cordgrass. Nubbins of luminous green saltwort are thrusting their way up through the exposed peat on the lower levels of the beach. Semi-palmated sandpipers, headed for Arctic nesting grounds, rise up out of the marsh and flit away. They cry in trilling whispers, while fog drifts in to cover the low white dunes of the nesting site.

I hear the deep, alarmed quacking of a black duck as it hurtles up out of a dark corner of the marsh, then the voice of a song sparrow, a spitting, spurting kind of melody. A few wintering Brant are still here, slowly working over the marsh, with a rolling gait. These small geese have beautifully shaped heads, like the geese painted and carved during the great ages of Egyptian art. But I miss the piping plovers, those pale, shy little birds of the dry sands, now a threatened species. I would see them occasionally, scuttling ahead and stopping, scuttling and stopping, in plover fashion, over the beach beyond where the terns nested. Vulnerable to disturbance, they have begun to disappear, literally turning into little ghosts, deprived of the protection their sandy-buff color would normally give them.

During the years when this colony was flourishing, I could hear it from a distance sounding like a great concentrated hive. When I walked toward them across the marsh, it was like coming to a wildly active bazaar, an outcry of foreign voices that grew louder the closer I came to it. Now a few loud scouts on the perimeter start to speed out and attack me, but the overall activity is far less intense because of a much smaller population.

On May 8, ten days after I had seen them arrive, I found the first dusty-brown, speckled eggs in their sandy scrape. After that, I spotted seven more nests with eggs. But in another two weeks, there were only some 40–50 birds left, out of an original 200 or more. The majority have abandoned the site, undoubtedly because of predators.

I found some tern feathers scattered around the fringes of the territory, possible evidence of a fox or a weasel, since their tracks have been found in the vicinity. For some years the colony has been harassed by the nocturnal raids of a great-horned owl, which would be enough to subdue the enthusiasm of any group of terns. Nightly desertion of nests means exposure of eggs and newly hatched chicks. In 1981, tern warden Peter Trull reported that an owl at this colony had been killing adult terns and sending the rest out over the water. As a result, the normal incubating period, a minimum of twenty-one days and an average of twenty-three, had been lengthened. It took an average of thirty days for the eggs to hatch, since five to eight hours passed each night while the terns were off their nests.

One year I was told by a friend, who had been out in his boat after dark, that he had seen a big flock of terns flying off the site at Gray's Beach, with much wild crying. They stayed out over the water for some time. I found evidence of the owl the next day in the form of the headless, torn bodies of a number of terns.

A hawk is less of a menace to a population than an owl, but if it lingers too long over a colony during the day, it can cause a constant state of anxiety. When a hawk comes into view, some terns will mob it, while others leave their nests to wheel out over the water and return. They will repeat this, time after time, until the enemy flies away.

A tern colony often seems like an armed camp, constantly on the alert, by day or night. They are preyed upon by owls, foxes, skunks, raccoons, and weasels, among others. Rats, where they occur, are a terrible menace. Occasionally a large garter snake, or a black racer, will swallow an egg or newly hatched chick. Even ants may get inside of an egg, if the shell has a hole in it, and destroy the embryo.

Predation is a fact of life, yet it is seldom consistent. If the great-horned owl leaves a colony alone early enough in the season, they may still be able to raise a fair percentage of their young. During any given nesting season, black-crowned night herons can raid a colony with devastating results, taking eggs and young, but they will be absent the following year. The short-eared owl, now an endangered species, normally foraging for meadow voles and other prey in grassy areas behind the dunes, will sometimes move in on a tern colony and destroy chicks. Foxes, which have adapted well to human presence and are at least temporarily on the increase, will steal down to the shore hunting for nests. Predators may become "specialists" in terns for periods of time, but their raids are not necessarily prolonged.

Since seabirds are normally long-lived, a population can withstand such ravages if they are not protracted. An adult pair of terns, during an average life span of twelve years, might only have to raise two or three chicks to maturity in order to maintain a population. Many individuals live a great deal longer than that. In 1988, a common tern first banded on Great Gull Island as a chick was found to be twenty-six years old. In 1970, Dr. Ian Nisbet found an Arctic tern in Maine that had been banded as a chick thirty-four years earlier. The annual mortality for terns averages between 10 and 12 percent. In small, unprotected colonies, few chicks survive, more often, none at all.

Gray's Beach, though successful for a number of years, was always limited in extent, being only some fifty yards wide and a hundred yards long. It has been even more reduced in size as a result of periodic storms. That, plus the persistence of predators, gradually forced the terns out, and they lacked the colony will to sustain them. The few pairs still nesting there are not numerous enough to sustain a strong defense and are being harassed by gulls. Further efforts to protect them are being made by the Massachusetts Audubon Society. They plan to put up an electric fence to discourage predators. Another year may see better results, encouraging further occupation of the site, but the colony has been much weakened.

It is likely that the terns moved on to join a much larger colony where they are better protected, because of their numbers as well as the aggressive action of the commons against intruders. One such colony now exists on Cape Cod's New Island, out in the waters of Nauset Marsh behind the Great Beach. The population has grown to 4,000 pairs, plus 1,000 pairs of laughing gulls that nest on the same site, in somewhat uneasy proximity, since these small, black-headed gulls are perfectly capable of preying on unprotected eggs and chicks in their midst.

Peter Trull and I visited New Island one afternoon several years ago. When we landed on its beach, the terns and gulls all rose into the air at once, a wing-swishing canopy of screaming birds. They too had been enduring nightly visits from a great-horned owl, which had left a brown, curled breast feather behind. Also lying on the sand were the sleek black heads and red bills of terns and laughing gulls. This may have unnerved them to an unnatural degree. If you did not know that they were constitutionally equipped to exist at a fairly high pitch at this time of year, you might have thought that in that tumultuous screaming there was a tone of mortal agony. I could distinguish the sharp alarm call of an occasional roseate out of the canopy over our heads. I also heard a rare Arctic, with a cry like a common's, but with a more rasping, nasal tone. All of them together sounded as one voice, of an extreme intensity, a racial protest against universal attrition. It contained an element of fear, which only their departure from the predatory land would finally relieve. A certain nervous fear, heightened by those ear-splitting cries, was also registering in me; it would have been intolerable if prolonged. Since we too could be classed as predators, dangerous to the colony's stability, we quickly left the island and returned by boat to the mainland.

Terns have been persecuted by man for centuries. Originally, native Americans took their eggs, although it seems to have had no appreciable effect on their overall population. It was an old custom among white fishermen and coastal dwellers to rob their nests in large quantities in the spring. To offset this, there seems to have been some local agreement in the North Atlantic that egging should not continue past June 10.

In 1870, as many as 100,000 terns were seen on a single beach off Nantucket Island, their immaculate sea-gray and white feathers stirring in the light. Yet the late nineteenth century was a period in which the terns began to be shot off for their feathers, which were sold to the millinery trade to adorn women's hats. At the same time, shorebirds were being killed in vast numbers by market gunners, until one species, the Eskimo curlew, was thought to be extinct, while others were brought to the brink of extinction. The massacre of terns continued all the way from Canada to Virginia, until their population was reduced to an all-time low. In Massachusetts, by 1890, there were only 5,000 pairs of common terns left, and 2,000 roseates. The destruction of terns, egrets, and shorebirds contributed to the enactment of conservation laws that led to an improvement. By 1920, the overall population of terns in Massachusetts had climbed to a total of 30,000–40,000 pairs.

The entire roseate population in the Northeast had only risen to 8,000 pairs, of which 6,000 were in Massachusetts. After that, roseates dropped in numbers until the present figure of 2,676 pairs. Less adaptable than the commons, they once thrived on remote islands they have since lost. They have been decimated in Europe, where a large population of gulls has been the major factor. At last count, the European population only amounted to 550 pairs. Off the waters of northern Britain, they have been further threatened in recent years by a precipitous decline in sand launces. This is their primary food, also vital for other seabirds such as puffins and skuas. The population of Arctic terns has also been seriously affected by the decline in this basic food.

Roseates nest within colonies of common terns, in heavy vegetation, or under the concealment of rocks, rubble, or driftwood. Because the nests of the commons are out in the open and conspicuous, their chicks suffer more from predators. Roseates also had the advantage over the other species in that they made a less easy target for the market gunners. Instead of bunching or flocking up when attacked, they flew off individually over the water. Also, they can bring in a more consistent supply of fish from offshore waters, without being as dependent as the commons are on inshore fluctuations.

Despite these apparent advantages, roseates are more likely to desert when disturbed. Their nature is less aggressive than the commons, warier and more flighty. So they have been more vulnerable. They are especially so now that their preferred sites, far from mainland disturbance and predators, have been lost to them.

By 1988, the number of common terns was rising fast, probably because of increased protection of their nesting sites and a drop in the gull population. Roseates were barely holding their own, and the leasts were slowly rising in Massachusetts from a low of 950 pairs in 1972. The Arctics, never very numerous in these latitudes to begin with, had never recovered from the plume hunters, and were down to 17 pairs.

With the great drop in tern populations, there followed a marked contraction in range. Most of the favorable islands were taken over by gulls. The growth of cities started the more recent fall of terns on our shores, and man's camp followers, the gulls, helped the process along. They have simply taken advantage of the mountains of waste that "progress" had made available to them, as well as offshore fishing operations. Like the terns, the fish are now disappearing, and with the increase in waste disposal facilities, the gulls too are at last declining, but they are hard to stop. Various unsuccessful efforts have been made, through shooting or poisoning, to relieve tern islands of their pressure. In a few local instances, where control measures were carefully and professionally applied, gulls were removed and the terns came back after deserting their sites. But a huge gull population still menaces tern eggs and chicks all along the shoreline, and probably will for a long time to come. Herring gulls at the turn of the century were very few in number along the Northeast coast, found in the northern part of New England. Their population, with the great black-backs catching up, exploded during this century. Their breeding range now extends to the Carolinas.

State, local, and federal agencies have been undertaking programs for the protection of terns throughout the Northeast, from Maine to New York, and they are beginning to come back. Despite such efforts, the roseates are still endangered. In the Northeast, as Dr. Ian Nisbet pointed out in his study of the Roseate tern,* "the species is becoming disturbingly concentrated in a few large colonies." They are primarily confined to two places where they are well monitored and protected, at Bird Island in Marion, Massachusetts, and at Great Gull Island off Long Island. If anything disastrous should happen to either one, through unexpected disturbance or gull predation, a large part of the population might be wiped out, and the remaining numbers would not be enough to sustain it.

As Dr. Nisbet has also pointed out, "human predation in the winter quarters has been the primary factor responsible for the decline in the regional population." Peter Trull, now education coordinator at the Cape Cod Museum of Natural History, visited coastal Guyana in recent years and saw terns being caught with nets. They were

---

*"Status and Trends of the Roseate Tern, *Sterna dougallii*, in North America and the Caribbean," prepared for the U.S. Fish and Wildlife Service, Office of Endangered Species, 1980.

thrown over the birds as they roosted at night on offshore banks. The terns were then sold for food in the market. The same is true of roseates off Ghana, Africa, where they are caught with snares set along a beach, or by means of a hook and line with fish as bait. Crowded out of territories in the north, killed during the winter, their options are continually narrowed down.

The dispossession of terns reflects a new and dangerous volatility in the earth environment. Populations forced out of synchronization with their habitats and sources of food have an unstable base to depend on. This is also true of us, who are both the cause and the victims of widespread, global displacements, and are only beginning to recognize that this round world and its spatially balanced communities of life is the only foundation for whatever stability we can claim for ourselves.

We and the herring gulls have been taking a parallel course, although they seem to be more prepared for the future than we are. One might admire them for their ability to take advantage of us or, on the other hand, pity us for our senseless wasting of a continent. As one who is neither a gull nor a tern but sees something of himself in both, my inclination is to help the homeless where I can.

On my Sunday trips to the dump, now a sanitary landfill and recycling center, I see few gulls as compared to what there used to be. There is not enough for them to eat. So I meet them down at the shore instead, where the living is better, except during a hard winter. They exist on a long-term footing with reality. Whatever happens as a result of our lopsided domination of the earth, the gulls are prepared for a thousand years more of feast and famine.

Our contemporary world favors the idea that there is no such thing as "nature" not made by man, or in his hands. To which the gulls, whose uncompassionate, yellow eyes regard me on the shore, might easily say: "Take your time. It's all you have, since you take everything, but do not seem to know what to do with it." The outcome lies not in us, but in areas of tolerance or rejection that belong to the deepest sense of earth.

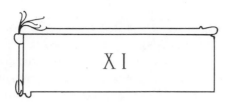

Eggs and Their Defenders

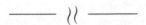

There is something about a seabird's exposure to all kinds of weather that attracts us. What they can tolerate, we often find unendurable and, at the same time, enviable. It is the same feeling that must have inspired John Muir to climb a tree during a snow storm and cling to it like a bobolink on a reed, or compelled the painter Joseph Turner to tie himself to a mast in order to experience a storm at sea.

Perhaps it was not only the terns I wanted to follow out at Gray's Beach, but the weather that ranged beyond it. This may be a vain occupation. Atmospheric motion, like the birds, has always left me behind; but it is the unencountered that sets us free. To watch a black-backed gull settling down comfortably in the trough of a wave on a freezing winter day keeps me in mind of my own limitations. But it also exposes me to the greater standards of the earth, and their powerful elusiveness.

The terns are now sitting on their eggs, during a growing number of warm days, in all their exposed locations along the shore. The buff and white sands are held down by runners of beach grass, whose limber, switching leaves serve as indicators of the force and direction of the wind. During hot days in June, the surface of the bare sand can reach extreme temperatures. When an egg is left exposed to the sun for only a brief length of time, it can destroy the embryo. Nesting terns have to brood their eggs and newly hatched young constantly in order to shade them. Incubation is not just a matter of warming the eggs, but of keeping them cool.

Low-lying sites can be washed out by flood tides. Wind-driven sands can cover nests and eggs. The Atlantic coast is periodically subjected to tropical hurricanes, which can be disastrous for the terns, especially if they hit early in the season. In June of 1972, hurricane Agnes moved up the coastline from Florida, while I was away in Maine. At the ternery off the salt marsh, the loss of eggs and chicks was about 50 percent.

I had experienced hurricanes on the Cape before. There was the early silence, heavy and dull, and then the distended roaring of the wind. The limbs of trees were cracking and falling; cutting sand was riding the air; the offshore waters seethed and boiled, while salt spray was driven right across the peninsula. I had thought of the terns on the day of the storm, wondering how they acted, how they endured. Perhaps many of them, forced off the ground, were riding it out, beating low over the marsh, while others managed to stay on their nests. Afterward I learned that the waves had broken over the low, frontal bluff of the island facing the beach, wiping out all the nests there. On the rear levels facing the marsh, the nests were flooded out. Only those on higher ground in the center survived.

When this hurricane passed New Jersey, observers saw common terns at one coastal site sitting on eggs during violent gusts, adjusting their plumage and their eggs as the sand kept piling up around them. The sand raised the level of some of the nests by seven centimeters.

The dedication of these terns to their nests is inspiring, and not less so because of their unconscious dependence on the weather. They pivot on its power and forbearance. A tern sitting on its eggs centers the year.

Although for most people eggs imply chickens, nothing more or less, a utilitarian food fit for utilitarian thought, the eggs of a wild bird service earth's desire. They are its perfected secret, with an orbital shape like the globe itself, their little lives destined for pitiless exposure, but hidden at this helpless stage from everything that could destroy them.

Eggs are also the method by which the earth distributes its progeny. A species of snail that moves from one stagnant pool to another over many inland miles, laying a train of eggs along the way, can travel proportionately as far as an Arctic tern, or a shorebird. To remain alive, every species must explore its environment, the property of the planet in its universal travel around the sun.

I can never find an egg, either nestled in the sand, on forest ground, or in some inland thicket, without thinking of it as an apex of the wild, the precious, the expendable. All the wild bird eggs I have ever seen are wonderfully subtle in their reflection of the ground that receives them. The eggs of terns are no exception. Their speckled shells are of rock and sky and summer sands, and of shadows woven by the grass.

One day I almost stepped on two tiny eggs, not more than an inch and a quarter long, as they suddenly materialized in the sand. They were at Popham Beach in Maine, just above the high-tide mark with its blackened, stringy seaweed, logs rafted in by storm tides, and bits of tawny and cloudy-gray driftwood. The tidewaters swirled around the great rocks lying offshore, carrying sea mists speared by sunlight. Only a few miles inland the world was covered by supermarkets, malls, condominiums, and continental asphalt taking its preoccupied traffic anywhere it wanted to go. These beige-colored, lightly speckled shiny spheres, only a little larger than pebbles, seemed uncommonly rare. No sooner had I caught sight of them than I looked away, and they had vanished.

Here was a semi-desert by the open ocean, with two nearly invisible eggs placed under the blazing scrutiny of the sky in nothing more than a shallow cup in the sand. It seemed to imply a lasting trust in the face of all finality. The fact is that least terns often lay their eggs so close to the tideline that they get washed away. If this happens early enough in the season, they will lay another clutch of eggs in exactly the same spot. This may sound stupid, implying a bird-minded reliance on repetitive behavior, but their choice of the upper levels of the beach to nest in comes out of a very long history. It was worked well enough, on balance, to keep the race alive. In a sense, we who have deserted our rhythmic alliance with the waves in favor of imposed regularity may not know half as much.

(It is interesting that in California, where least terns are endangered, they are, at the same time, holding their own, especially where their sites are protected. Leasts also seem to adapt fairly well to human presence where it does not overwhelm them. They can nest back of a summer beach covered over with sun bathers, picnickers, and volleyball players, but they still require their own space. Their level of site fidelity is also higher in California than on the east coast because of the milder climate. Far less severe storms occur there to cause drastic changes in the coastline so that birds can anticipate more consistency. Changes in the environment affect reactions in a bird's fundamental biology, though it is hard to judge just how severe they have to be to make the birds move from year to year.)

Leasts are much smaller and far less aggressive than the commons or Arctics, and depend on their size and inconspicuous coloration to keep them hidden. All the same, these active, yellow-billed little birds, with a white patch on their foreheads that shines in the sunlight, can be fiercely protective. (The patch is like a signal. Perhaps it helps them to recognize each other from a distance.) On Popham Beach, I saw one chasing a herring gull which had come too close to its nest. It was a very uneven contest in terms of size. Yet the little tern went right after the gull and managed to get close enough to dislodge a white feather, which eddied gently to the ground.

Learning to tell the difference between eggs may not seem to be a matter of monumental importance to most of us, unless it has some practical advantage, but the more we reduce the earth's diversity, the more vital such exercises become. The wild egg is earth's signature, a sign of inerasable distinction; it belongs to no world dominated by a single race, but to a multiplicity of them, each a facet of creation, in a flowing, enveloping universe.

The egg of a roseate, which only lays one as a rule and occasionally two, is likely to be paler than that of a common, with two or three eggs in a clutch. It is slightly more pointed and with finer, less blotchy speckles and spots, tending to form a ring at one end. The eggs of the Sandwich tern, of Europe and our southern coastline, are usually very pale in color as the chicks will be, and often a creamy white, with black markings on them like some still indeciphered calligraphy. They are larger than those of the commons or roseates and more conical in shape.

On the other hand, I believe there is no really reliable way of distinguishing between the eggs of common and Arctic terns, though there may be enough of a difference here and there to encourage professionals to keep on trying to prove it. Coloring, incidentally, may vary with locality. I have heard that in the high-Arctic regions of Greenland, Arctic terns lay eggs that are considerably darker than in the more southerly parts of the country.

Eggs in the same nest may vary a great deal. One might be a pale blue, or bluish-green, while the one next to it is a cloudy-brown. The same female, by the way (and this is also true of other birds such as oystercatchers), will come back year after year to the same site and lay eggs with the same variations in color. Chicks in the same nest can be quite different in color. I have seen two baby leasts together, one with grayish down and the other a light nut-brown.

The color of the egg may be related to the behavior of the bird. The whitish egg of the Sandwich and, to a lesser extent, of the roseate, is more conspicuous than the egg laid by an Arctic, a common, or a least. This is partly compensated for by the habit of Sandwich terns of nesting in dense colonies, as roseates did when they were more numerous. Sandwich terns also defecate around their nests instead of walking away from them, as a common tern will do. This makes their nests easier to see; nor do they carry the eggshells away, like the other species. All this would seem to heighten the danger from predators, but Sandwich terns do not leave their nests when a hawk or a gull flies over, but stay where they are. The Arctics and commons have a different form of protection. Their nests are scattered rather than concentrated, so the birds fly up and distract intruders by attacking them, while the uncovered eggs are well camouflaged, and so are the chicks.

So the egg lies exposed, bare but blended in, in the way of each hunting beak, claw, or set of teeth, of each skunk, fox, or owl. It has to be covered from the burning eye of the sun and the violent dangers of the weather. Yet this means trust of a kind, which men may share with terns. Do we not, in our unconscious, trust the withholding of tides that might inundate us?

After the eggs are laid, they are continuously incubated, except when an intruder comes to the ternery, or a spontaneous panic occurs, or when the birds leave their nests to defecate. Males and females share, to a varying extent, in sitting on the eggs but, to begin with, the female spends more time at it than the male. When the female is finished laying eggs and begins to incubate them, it is a period when she needs to regain her strength, and for some days she is fed at the nest by her mate. This is a critical period for her, and for the future of the nest, and it goes better with a good provider. As time goes on, both sexes share in foraging for food to a varying extent, and then in feeding the chicks. After the chicks start hatching out, activity over the colony becomes much more intense. There is much loud and busy flying back and forth between the nests and the outlying waters.

Changing over at the nest is a ceremony in itself. A male may bring a fish to a female at the nest. They posture, bowing and bending, inclining heads and necks upward as in courtship. When he has no fish, she begs for it. There are guttural, throaty sounds of "kohrr-kohrr" or "kurr-kurr-kurr" as they reply to each other. They are both restless in each other's presence and toward the need for continuous incubation of the eggs. After the male begins to share in nest sitting, the two change over with no particular regularity. A male may sit on the nest for hours, or only minutes, while the female stands by, resting and waiting her turn. One of a pair may fly in, prompting the mate to leave the nest, but if the first does not settle in and start brooding right away, the other will often come back again.

Before it leaves them, a bird that has been sitting on the eggs often indulges in preening gestures, or it plucks at grass and sticks around the nest, tossing them over its shoulder or passing them along its feathers. This has been interpreted as showing a conflict between a strong desire to brood the eggs and a contrary urge to leave them. As a result of this picking and strewing around of grass and sticks, a nest scrape will gather quite a good deal of material around it which the birds never put there intentionally.

There is a fussiness, with much adjusting, when a tern settles down on its eggs. It will often make a motion of tucking or nudging them under its ventral feathers, and experiments show that it will do this even when the eggs have been removed. The position of the egg in the nest is very important to them because they are adjusting eggs against their bare brood patch, a highly sensitive area of skin on their bellies. Gulls and terns are not averse to sitting on substitute eggs made of wood or plastic. They do not seem to be able to tell the difference at first, but the exact position of the eggs seems essential.

(Watching a film of nesting fairy terns on an island in the Indian Ocean, I saw at least one reason why the birds themselves, aside from the weather, did not dislodge their eggs from their precarious perches. A fairy tern, coming back to incubate its one egg that sat out on a bare and narrow branch, moved up and over it with natural lightness and instinctive care. It hardly touched the egg until it settled down on top of it. In a tropical climate, it may also be its habit to crouch over an egg in order to shade and cool it.)

Watching terns at their nests, preferably from a blind, is a great pleasure to me. I listen to their croupy, velvety talk. I watch them posturing as they leave their nests or come back to them, and I listen to them crying to one another as they fly off. When a tern exchanges places with its mate and settles down on the eggs, adjusting its pure gray feathers, the tail feathers crossed behind it, its gestures are as protective as any I have ever seen. Regardless of how erratic or ambivalent they may appear to be on the surface, these birds have an inborn composure on the nest which is as old as the world.

When coming in to a nesting area, an intruder is met by screams of alarm and outrage. Common terns will fly at your head, with a low "ahn-ahn-ahn-ahn" of annoyance at first that turns into a rasping, staccato "kek-kek-kek-kek-kek." Occasionally, one of them may hit you on the head and draw blood. They will also let their droppings fly at you in their excitement. Because some of them are expert dive bombers, it is wise to wear a hat. Roseates, on the other hand, are less aggressive. They will make low, flying approaches, sounding a slightly less harsh "kaagarrh-kaarh," but they veer off before they reach you.

Those who have to walk through a ternery must watch their feet so as not to step on eggs. They must also move steadily forward, or the birds will be kept too long from their nests. Intrusions by beach parties, picnickers, or by people oblivious to the needs of the birds can cause them to desert if carried on too long. Unleashed dogs running wildly through a colony, killing chicks and keeping adults in the air, can endanger its existence. Because of our sprawling summer population covering the beaches, it became increasingly difficult to keep such disturbances in check. Conscious protection became a necessity, and is proving to be more effective as time goes on. "Keep Off—Nesting Birds" is one of the more critical signs you will ever see. As a result of a growing number of tern wardens and conservation measures undertaken by state and local authorities, a great many more people are now aware of what it means.

Some individuals are more militant than others. A male at Great Gull Island used to tear around a corner to attack any visitor or member of the staff who showed up, and a few people found it downright exasperating. To some extent, familiarity breeds contempt in terns. Aggressiveness in some of them becomes almost automatic toward people they have become accustomed to.

A great deal is made of their ties to a territory when tern behavior is discussed, but aggressiveness is not always limited by home

~

boundaries. A friend of mine and his son were out in a rowboat on a Cape Cod pond, where no terns were nesting within several miles, and one dove down and pecked the boy on the back of the head. This only means, I suppose, that aggression is an attribute of the nesting season, but not always confined to a nest.

Once I caught sight of a harbor seal swimming offshore. When the terns along the shoreline spotted its head, they all flew off over the water and circled it. Individuals dove out of the flock and sheared over the animal, much as they do when centering on a school of fish. When the seal swam off at a distance that satisfied them, they all returned to the shore, crying and posturing.

Herring and black-back gulls can be roosting on the edge of a colony, on dune edges or offshore rocks, and not arouse the terns at all. But if one gull flies over the territory, transgressing a boundary understood by them, they will attack and drive it off.

Females as well as males act aggressively during the season. They all do, including chicks at an early age, although the adult males assume the role of defenders with greater intensity. Unless forewarned, people attacked by terns for the first time hardly know how to react.

On the Farne Islands, just off the British coast, the warden told me that some visiting school children who had seen Alfred Hitchcock's film *The Birds* on television had been very apprehensive. They thought they might be attacked by savage terns when they landed on the island where they nested. In that nervous frame of mind, one small boy had an encounter with an Arctic tern, whose nest was quite close to a roped-off path that led up the steep bank from the water. I watched while the fierce little black-capped bird with its blood-red bill began to swoop back and forth above his head, which had a dark blue, schoolboy's cap of its own. The boy was startled at first and ready to run, but valor won out. He suddenly put his fists up and began to duck and dance as if he was in a boxing ring, all the while yelling loud threats. Both parties disengaged after that, their honor intact.

A biographer of Rose Fitzgerald Kennedy,* tells how Kennedy and her father, the noted politician "Honey Fitz," were once strolling on the beach and were attacked by terns, which must have had nests nearby. Honey Fitz was outraged by the arbitrary pests and appealed to the selectmen of the town of Hyannis for assistance. They in turn brought in the local conservation officer, who tried to scare off the birds by firing blanks at them, only to have them swoop away and come back again, fearlessly and repeatedly. It was then suggested to some state office that the birds be shot. Luckily there were federal laws against it. Fitzgerald, the former mayor of Boston, then threatened to appeal to the federal government to have the law overruled. Since then, it has become far less likely that such *force majeure* could succeed. But that self-concentrated tide we call progress is still inclined to tolerate nature only when it is not in its way. Estrangement from the land inspires the ignorant to demand guaranteed protection against its life. The army is called out to deploy their helicopters against a mosquito, just as wolves became the victims of our myths about their depravity.

For the average person coming in on an Arctic or common tern colony for the first time, it is their aggressiveness that seems the most obvious. This might be something to admire, "the brave little birds," or to detest. I have heard both reactions. Whether or not we like terns, however, we cannot help being struck by the vehement nature with which creation has endowed them. They seem to be almost constantly quarrelsome, or on the verge of it. The distinctions they make between friend and enemy seem none too clear. In their nervous agitation, they appear to have very little leeway. They are narrowly concentrated, readily alarmed, immediately dependent on outer stimuli.

This is the way, of course, that we see them on the nesting grounds. As fishing flocks during the rest of the year, they behave entirely differently. During the spring and summer season, all their actions reflect what they have to contend with: weather, predators, the short-

* Gail Cameron, *Rose* (New York: Putnam, 1971).

ness of time. It is inescapable, but it is also an exercise in daring. In the interests of an assured future, they practice strict ritual and ceremony, and it is done with emotion. They are always on guard, always using the time they have to relate to their territories on a life and death level, before they move on. It is an admirable race, and there is nothing to be gained in denying that it has any lessons for us.

The Speech of Terns

For most people, animals speak with a rudimentary voice. When you hear pigeons cooing in the city park, you are certainly inclined, as I once was, to think of them as little more than dumb birds, with nothing to say. This was before I learned that their senses had more capabilities than I knew how to express. Behind the outer details that we pass by each day lies a vast range of perception and communication.

It is easy enough to think that a distinctive species like a bird, with one recognizable call, must lack individuals. This has been disproved by a great many observers. That birds are individuals is now accepted by any student of their behavior. During the nesting season, certainly, when terns can be watched and listened to, they show marked differences in traits. One bird will be unusually militant, another more passive. Some adults are better parents than others, and will go on feeding their young for longer periods of time. Many are simply incompetent. They wander off and stop feeding the half-grown juveniles before they are able to fend for themselves. This is a society with considerable differences in skill and temperament. In their own fashion, they display almost as many vagaries as we do.

I seldom know how to interpret their constant interchanges, which can be just as quiet and subtle as they are loud. The motivation behind what terns are expressing to each other, in tones of varying intensity, is not easily grasped. This unique race has a vocal ability which might have some passing resemblance to a jarring, musical instrument. Yet in terms of the basic urgencies of life, the call rings true. At the very least, with a complicated social structure, and a complex relationship to the changing facets of their surrounding world, the terns are not ones to give us examples in easy, animal simplicity. And just as water, land and air are constantly changing around them, interpretations of their behavior can never be expected to be final. There is an electric speech between any life and its environment which goes unheard.

I have often felt an element of offhandedness, or absent-mindedness, in their behavior, as if they were waiting on each other's signals before they acted. Now and then a tern seems to land almost forgetfully with a fish. It looks around and then flies away with it again. Or one bird will approach another and then break off contact, as if lacking the stimulus to follow through with whatever action it has started to perform. "One often gets the impression," wrote Niko Tinbergen in *The Herring Gull's World*, "that birds call when they are strongly motivated by an internal urge, and yet cannot satisfy that urge by proclaiming the activities to which it drives them." Calls are outlets for impulses and emotions which often require the right signals to set them off, so terns can appear to be highly ambivalent.

It is not so much that terns are always indecisive, but that they spend much time, as Tinbergen also put it, "in half-hearted, incomplete movements, before any unambiguous, overt act is performed." They have a limited set of these "urges," such as the need to copulate, to brood the eggs and young, to change over at the nest, or to forage for food, and these require the right situation. Like us, they often find it difficult to switch too quickly from one activity to another. If the bird is only half-hearted about its inner motivation, it will not carry through, but the stronger the feeling, the more direct the action.

To the human outsider, tern society may seem to have its contradictions, though that is preferable to thinking that nothing is going on of any significance. "Group adherence" on the territory has very little to do with "love." Antagonism, or something that resembles a case of aggressive jitters, seems permanent. So, if there is no love between them, how do they cooperate? During the nesting season, the outward evidence of cooperation is between pairs and when they flock together to mob intruders. Otherwise, their relationships look very edgy indeed. On the other hand, they are, at the very least, preoccupied with each other. Being highly territorial birds, terns nest in places which are as deeply mapped in them as their timing to the season. They are magnetically drawn to their nesting sites, though they can desert them in the face of disaster, and move to alternate ones if there is time. A common order is created out of underlying tension and that spontaneity which is so characteristic of them. Anger, distress, fear, and alarm are basic emotions they all share and signal to one another. Each cry or compulsive act can radiate out to others in the immediate vicinity, or spring the whole colony into action.

Terns communicate with high, harsh, sea-reflecting voices. Their tonal range is considerable. They may scream with excitement or descend into low, throaty comments at the nest. Their calls, as distinct from those of male song birds on their territories whose singing can be long, complex, and elaborate, are short and emphatic. Gulls are said to have some ten distinct, recognizable calls. It is possible that the highly vocal and expressive terns may have more, though the variety of intonations behind the call escapes us for the most part.

In crows, on the other hand, some 300 separate calls have been found. The raven too, which Konrad Lorenz mentioned as the only bird he knew that could use a human word for conscious purposes, is a bird of such varied eloquence, so full of whim, sardonic and knowing behavior, that it filled the world of myth with stories about it. Crows and ravens have large brains in proportion to their body weight, which may explain their intelligence. Of course, this is a profound source of gratification to us whose brains are proportionately still larger, whether or not our use of them yields intelligent results. Where we lag behind the birds is probably in a superior quality of awareness, a responsive relationship to this sentient earth which we have been shamefully neglecting.

In the process of making ourselves the measure of things, we do not widen out the world so much as confine it. If man is the mirror, then all animals are defined through his sight, and that greater space in which they participate with such intricate style becomes subordinated to our exclusive use of it. I am suspicious of our comparisons of mental ability. What do we really know of mind in the first place? The mind and voice of the tern belong to a sphere we have hardly begun to respect. They know space who speak its magic.

Through their calls, terns convey information to each other, at times almost diffidently, and at others with considerable feeling. There is no mistaking the rapid, staccato cry they use when attacking an intruder, especially when it is yourself. It culminates with a wild shriek of "ahk!" "ahrk!" or "karr!" and at this pitch of excitement, they loose their droppings on your head.

Some of the calls of a common tern sound both strident and silvery, others harsh and deep. Still others seem to be little more than casual, absent-minded note takings, which may verge abruptly into high-pitched exclamations. It is always difficult to rely on written symbols for describing bird calls. It was pointed out to me, some years ago, that the "keearh" or "keeurh" call by which the common tern is known can also be heard as a nasal "ayhurr-ahn-ahn-ahn."

The most elaborate calls are made by birds advertising for their mates. A male cries out with a "keera!" or "keeyer!" to the female. Later on, during the early period of house hunting or establishing a nest, terns call "korkorkor" while posturing before making a scrape in the sand. Adults carrying in food proclaim it with a "keeyer," or "kitikeeyer." A bird flying by with a fish may utter a noncommittal

~

"ketuh-ketuh," whereas one being furiously chased by others intent on robbing it will give a hysterical "kekearr!" of distress. The alarm call is a short "chik," or "chip"; with roseates this is "chivy" or "chewik." An abrupt "k-kaah" may accompany a brief flurry with another bird passing in flight.

They often sound as if they were making announcements about presentations, departures and arrivals, things to fly away from, things to be attacked. They may have a separate alarm call for a hawk flying overhead, for a man approaching with a dog, or a dog without a man. They seem to say, "I have something" (such as a fish), or "Move over," "Keep away" or "Give," all fundamental statements. Other than their distinct, recognizable calls, their cries vary a great deal depending on the circumstance. Human language is obviously much more versatile and complex than all this similar vocalizing. Yet what may sound very limited to us hides a wealth of gesture and response which is no less complex in its nature. If terns do not seem to employ conscious meaning with much elaboration, they still mean like mad, as those of us who listen are fully aware. Theirs is a language which is intensely felt, and joins a universal realm of symbolic communication which goes deeper than thought.

Ceremony and domesticity often go together. In that, at least we can recognize ourselves. We need rhythm, design, and common ritual in our lives, whether in sports, the dance, or at the family table. Common terns during nest relief seem to "talk" to each other. The female begs rapidly at first, with a "ki-ki-ki-ki," after which her mate may bring her a fish. They will both utter a low "keeyer." The male addresses her with that rapid "korr-korr-korr," which changes into a croupy "kuh-kuh-kuh-kuh." The sounds he makes are hoarse and watery, as if coming from somewhere down in a pipe, and change to a remarkable degree. A bird leaving its replacement behind at the nest may make a slight "tik-tik" as it plucks at some grass—a nervous relief from tension, and then a louder "tik-tik-tik-tik" as it flies away.

Although we classify birds as being among the higher vertebrates, we are still very wary of crediting them with mental and emotional capabilities which are anything like ours. But without some insight into our own emotions and states of mind, it would not be possible to understand their behavior at all.

Birds do not dwell on the mysteries. Ideas are foreign to them. But when I hear that sharp-edged tern voice again, striking across the sea-skimming air like a bell, I have no reason to think that I am superior to them. They lift my senses and my state of being into the company of the elect. What kind of an environment is it which we are only able to judge on our own terms?

Can birds be acquiring information through senses we know nothing about? It is clear enough that in some not too limited ways, they see more of the world than we do. If the quality of the marine environment is in their speech and searching lives, then it lies behind their perception. I watch them from a shore that looks out on a sea of awareness, wave after wave passing over infinite stretches of time with such majestic order as to elude the calculating mind.

XIII

Hunger

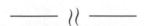

Several days before a tern chick emerges from the egg, a "starring" can be seen on the shell. Then a small hole appears with the tip of a bill, the "egg tooth," beginning to break through. About a day after that, the chick is hatched, waggling its head in a weak fashion, damp at first, though the down dries quickly. While the egg is hatching, the parents act in a nervous and uneasy way. At times, ants enter the cracked egg at this stage and start to destroy the chick. (I have heard of an account of a female least tern's extreme agitation when a swarm of red ants had moved in to attack an egg in her nest.) Once a chick is finally out of the egg, the parents are reluctant to leave the nest at all, even during an alarm, since chicks are at a very delicate and fragile period of their existence. The newborn are unable to regulate their own temperature and have to be constantly brooded.

On a hot day in late June, the leaves of the beach pea are folded to reduce evaporation and conserve moisture and the beach grasses, gently switching in light airs, glisten in the sun above the gush and stir and backfalling of the waves. Since they have no sweat glands to

evaporate moisture, parent terns sit on their nests with open beaks
and vibrating throats, known to science as "gular fluttering." A male
flies in to one of the nests and tries to deliver to its two- or three-
day-old chick a fish that is much too big and slippery for it. After
gaping and reaching in a futile way toward the food, held in the
parent's bill, the chick is unable to pick it up when it is dropped on
the ground. So the adult flies off, to return later on with another
offering of a more manageable size. Meanwhile the female sitting on
the nest has picked up the fish out of the sand and eaten it herself.

This sequence occurs fairly often, because a male common tern
begins to bring fish in to a chick from a half an hour to an hour after
it has hatched. He may also feed the female at this stage. At first, the
fish he brings in may be too big for the chick, as if he was not able
to discriminate between what it needs and what his mate requires.
But the male usually learns to adjust, and a great deal depends on
it. Otherwise the chick may starve. These early hours and days of
feeding are vital. For a poorly fed chick, there is no second chance.

Sandwich and roseate terns have access to a more dependable
supply of fish in deeper waters, and they seem to be more selective
than the commons when feeding newly hatched chicks. They start
with a fish of a manageable size, and bring in larger ones as the
chick grows. The common is much more random about it. It may
produce a small inshore minnow or pipefish, bits of shrimp or crab
larvae, even insects, and then return with a silversides or sand eel
later on. The reason dead fish are so often found in a ternery is that
these are the ones that have proved to be too much for the chicks to
swallow.

The little fawn chicks are cryptically colored, like the eggs they
come from. The markings on their bodies, with lines and patches
like light debris on a beach, tend to draw your eye away from them.

"I am not here," says the chick, cast out onto a hungry planet.
From the beginning, the chick crouches on the nest in a submissive
posture when it is frightened. After a few days, it has grown enough
to be able to move a short distance from the nest when disturbed.
As it grows still older and larger, able to scuttle and run, it finds

nearby hiding places in grass, seaweed, beach heather, or rocky crevices. These give better, and cooler, cover than the original nest; and it is there that the adults now go to feed them.

Baby least terns will run off at any intrusion and head for a sheltering hollow. On a sandy beach, this is all too often part of a rut made by a beach buggy, those off-the-road vehicles that have been able to use the beaches as highways. The result, especially at night, is that chicks get run over, or scattered abroad to be picked up by predators. Controlling these vehicles has been a major problem in areas where the terns nest. That many such places have been turned into sanctuaries, or posted and roped off, does not always satisfy those who feel the beach is theirs. Tern wardens spend more of their tact and energy in trying to educate the public than they do on the routine task of protecting the birds themselves. The gap is still very wide between our assumed right of possession and the common struggle to live. With eternal vigilance, enough people to make a difference may eventually be persuaded that we and the little terns crouch down in the same tire tracks, in common danger. We have no prior rights. A deeper logic moves us all.

A tern's uneasiness toward the predatory land shows itself in the chick. In nesting grounds that are located above a beach, half-grown birds, and at times much younger ones, will occasionally hurry off toward the water after being seriously disturbed. In Denmark, I saw a chick run across the beach and take to the water after a family and their dog had routed it out of its hiding place in the grass, though I don't believe they knew it was there or the dog would have chased it. It swam fairly readily, though tidal currents seemed to be carrying it away from the shore. I could only hope it would not be gobbled up by a gull and that it would survive immersion.

Adult terns float in the water and bathe in it for brief periods. On a hot afternoon, I have often seen small flocks splashing in the sea, then moving on after a few seconds to another spot, where I could see them ducking their heads in and beating their wings as they bathed. But they are poor swimmers, their feet being too small to propel them efficiently, and prolonged immersion will drown them.

I have noticed that common terns on rocky islands find it slippery and tippy going as they cross over stony ground to reach their nests, their wings doing most of the maneuvering. Arctics, with even smaller feet, move, as it is appealingly described in the *Audubon Encyclopedia of Birds,* with a "mouselike glide."

From the first time I first saw an egg chipped by a living thing inside it, then watched the chick emerging, I felt drawn by a new level of urgency in the colony. It was being repeopled by its ardent parents. The young are now exposed to the world and highly vulnerable. Everything centers on their need to be fed and protected. Parental fishing expeditions continually shuttle back and forth. The nests are intensely defended. When a stranger, not its mate, lands too close to a bird that is brooding its new chicks, it is immediately threatened with attack. As the chicks grow, leaving the nest and moving out to new hiding places or open areas where they wait to be fed, the parents defend them there. The speed with which these tiny young move out and express themselves seems almost violent. They soon take on some of the scrappy character of their race. As the days go by, they become increasingly militant toward each other when competing for food or even, in an erratic way, toward adult strangers that may intrude on their space. They are full of the growing emotions of defensiveness and alarm.

A three- or four-day-old chick hides under a piece of driftwood a foot or so away from its nest after having been disturbed. When one of the parents return, it comes out and scuttles back to the nest. The female parent turns toward the little one, stretching her wings, shivering and fluffing up her feathers. She then takes it under her protection, cloaking it in the classic way, tail feathers crossed behind her body.

On a sandy shore, with its growth of beach plants and grasses, a varied, uneven terrain marked also by hollows, driftwood, and thatch flung in by the tides, the nests are so spaced that you can understand how chicks might be found and identified. Each square foot has its own individuality. But when the young begin to move away, how is it possible for the parents to find them without an exhaustive search?

The answer to it lies in the voice. Every parent knows the call of its own chick.

That every nesting pair of tens of thousands of sooty terns on a featureless tropical beach, or of any other tern species, could recognize its young seems astonishing at first. Perhaps we imagine that a tribe with only one uniform could have only one voice. But even before a chick is hatched, parent birds can hear its faint peeping inside the shell. They react to it by shortening their absences, so that whichever parent is attending to the nest when the chick finally emerges will be better prepared to feed it. Some days after that, when the chick has left the nest, a parent coming in with food is able to locate it by its insistent, rapid, high-pitched tones. Adults in turn call to their young so that they learn to recognize the parental voice.

Terns in effect choose from the infinitely varied modulations of the living world. So it should not surprise us who play on the variations of language, and a perpetual store of musical invention, that this sensitivity should be a common property of life. Recognition through tone of voice is as central to the life of a tern as it is to our own.

During the first few days of their existence, chicks are continually brooded by their parents, with the female taking the greater share, and this seems to be the period in which specific recognition begins. After about five days, when both parents may be off fishing instead of at the nest, they and the chicks will have learned each other's voices. The petulant cries of their offspring appear to stimulate the adults when they return. Even so, when the chicks are dispersed and in hiding, it may take the parents some time to find them. They have to come out and beg vociferously in order to be recognized.

A parent flies in with a fish to a nest from which a chick has wandered away, and seems not to know where to find it. Perhaps the chick has failed to respond to its call. So it ends up eating the fish itself. As it flies in, a parent common tern cries out with its individual intonation of "keeyer," meaning, "Here's a fish." The chicks normally start up from where they are dozing and digesting in the sunlight to beg insistently. At a very early age, they may beg from adults who are not their parents, so it may be that recognition is more strongly developed after they are a week or two old. After that, they may be able to hear a parent when hidden from view, or when their eyes are closed.

A female parent broods the chicks in the nest. After a while, her mate flies in, prior to a changeover, solicitiously poking under her wings, as if to inquire after their welfare, though it is more likely that he is coaxing her to move off and let him take his turn. I have often felt that there must be a profoundly domestic tale to be put together out of countless minor incidents such as this. Other distractions take me away too soon. Chance acquaintance is never enough.

Domestic life in the human race, with all its intricate, long-term relationships, each child and adult in a family with their own sphere of reality, hardly compares with this short, seasonal race for existence. What can a time sense mean to a bird? Internal rhythms move it. Every day it responds to changes in the intensity of light and temperature, as it does to the weather at large. The successions of day and night govern its actions as, of course, they do our own. Their annual rhythm corresponds to seasonal change, and controls the time and direction of their migration. This is the governing world we hypothesize for them, as opposed to ourselves, but, like us, they have to answer to commands that were never self-originated, in the common frame of hunger and birth.

There is a suspicion that young, unmated birds that show up on a territory may not be there simply because they followed a colony as it settled in. They may be returning to sites where they last heard a parental voice. It is in *place* that life starts out and is sustained in the memory. We have hardly begun to understand or appreciate the family interactions of these birds.

Terns' fierce efforts to nurture their young in the face of constant danger and attrition has qualities we can relate to. During exceptionally hot summer days, when the surface temperature of the sandy ground is extreme, chicks may easily expire, even when covered by a parent. But the parent terns often fly out over the water, dip in and wet their wings so as to cool them and their young. There is no need, in this context, to quibble about conscious versus unconscious intent.

From the start, when a chick is able to utter no more than a thin peep, it quivers with the desire for food, holding out the tiny stumps that will soon grow into wings. In a few days, it is fairly hopping with hunger, and is now the center of tribal attention. The "ki-ki-ki-ki" or "gli-gli-gli-gli" of its begging are beginner's notes in the practice of existence. In a couple of weeks, these cries will have turned into something like a staccato "argh-argh-argh-argh," which give way to a more varied range of calls as the birds grow. It is not hard to interpret the rattling voice of a chick as it struts, jumps, and dances like a wayward child in a rage: "I will be heard!"

It seems likely that a shortage of food causes chicks to try and steal food from each other with greater enthusiasm since they are aggressively hungry. They will often engage in tugs of war, with a fish in the middle. They start out in the practice of life with as much native intensity as the rest of their kind, ready to take on an unrelenting future. Occasionally, a young tern feathered out enough to fly around by itself, but not old enough to have learned how to fish, will desert its home territory for another area where chicks are being fed. There it will hang around until a parent flies in with food for its own young. Then it rushes out to try and intercept the fish before it reaches its rightful recipient.

(At times there may be a shortage of parental care, even in a healthily occupied colony. If numbers are high, many terns will be flocking offshore competing for fish. This means that they spend more time away from their young. The result is that chicks move around and try to get adopted by other parents. This wandering, in other words, is not due so much to lack of food as it is to inattentive parents. As it goes with much in the seasonal life of the terns, a social order that seems vigorous and resilient at any given period may also have an element of instability.)

Hunger and a tern chick are synonymous. As you listen to their insistent calls, or watch them at an early stage coming out of the shelter of a parent's wing to swallow a fish, jerking their heads back and gulping hard as it goes down, you know "I want! I want!" is the most fundamental cry in all the world.

The appetite and capacity of a chick in its first few days of life is prodigious. Even those fish that are not too big for it to swallow look outsized. It is perhaps comparable to a man gulping down a steak one third his size. The adult presenting a fish to its young will hold it close to the head, so that a chick receives it that way. Occasionally, the young will gag and choke when they try to eat a fish tail first. The chick pecks toward the food as a parent holds it, then grabs and pulls it away, starting to swallow with its head held back. This pink-beaked, downy ball of expectancy may be seen with a fish tail hanging out of its mouth, while the rest is being digested inside. Complete digestion of a fish small enough to swallow down whole might take the chick no more than about twenty minutes.

Even an average requirement in tern young of a few ounces of fish a day would add up to many pounds by the time it is fledged. I imagine that in a colony of thousands, the overall food requirement could be measured by the ton.

I concentrated on the feeding routine for a nest that contained a pair of chicks, four or five days old, one a little larger than the other. The larger chick was fed a sizable fish at 10:30 A.M., and the other got nothing. At 11:40, a parent brought in another good-sized fish which the smaller one took, only to have it grabbed by its nest mate. At 11:58, the smaller one took a medium-sized fish, perhaps because its sibling was stuffed for the moment and lacked interest. Then at 12:48 P.M., a larger fish was brought in and offered to the small chick, but the big one snatched it away again.

At 1:12 P.M., just before I left to feed myself, the small-sized chick was offered some bits of food I could not identify from a distance, and promptly swallowed them. I never learned whether the pair was successfully reared or not. The amount fed to chicks in any given nest may average out, so that they are equally nourished. Under certain conditions though, one chick may be fed less than the others and be stunted in the process. The feeding tempo might be interrupted, for example, if the parents took longer than usual to get food, because of competition, or because of several stormy days in a row. In that event, the largest chick might be fed to the neglect of a smaller one. Of course, the size of fish varies considerably with the kind available, not only from day to day and week to week, but from one year to the next.

The voracity of chicks is vital to them and their species. For a creature that is able to fly by the time it reaches thirty days, more or less, the imperative is never to stop growing. The physical and nervous crises this would entail for human beings if they grew at a commensurate rate does not bear thinking about. Change is visible in the chicks from day to day. With my ear next to them all the while, I might be able to hear them rustling like growing corn on a summer's night.

During its first three days of existence, a chick doubles its weight, and in four more days doubles it again, and again about eleven days after that. Then the curve begins to level off. In other words, the rate of feeding has to increase as the young continue to grow, although they consume relatively more to begin with and grow faster than they will later on.

While the young are very small, the shuttling back and forth of the adults is continuous. At times, the food they bring in does not seem to be acceptable. I have seen a parent common tern fly in with a pipefish and then, having no chick emerge from a sheltering wing, leave again with an air of "What am I going to do with this?"

When a chick drops a fish, the parent that brought it in may only fly away, but just as often it is picked up and presented once more. I have seen a bird watching with what looked like a patiently critical eye while its mate tried to reduce a freshly caught fish to a manageable limpness, after its chick was unable to get a grip on it. But then the parent gave up, swallowed the fish itself, and flew out low across the water, dipping its bill in to clean it. Occasionally, an adult flies off with a fish after a chick has dropped it on the ground, dips it into the water to wash it and returns to the nest to try again.

So they race through the tidal summer, seeing to family needs. While the young are being brooded or fed, and some eggs still incubated, crowds of inactive terns may still be resting and loafing along the shores of the territory. Some of these unattached birds may be dozing, with their bills neatly tucked inside their wings, or engaged in the half-hearted motions of courtship. When a new bird comes into land among them, it is greeted with upward stretching heads and bills.

On the nesting grounds, any tern coming in with a fish may be furiously chased by other birds trying to take it away. It has to race, swoop, dash back and forth until it gives its pursuers the slip and lands at the nest, or the place where its young are waiting. I have seen a tern come in with a fast rush, another bird hard on its tail, and drop the fish just as it reached the chick, which rushed out and grabbed it. This kind of action excites all the birds in the vicinity. Parents stand over their young in protective attitudes, others cry out, posture, or fly up. Even if the fish carrier is not chased, its arrival is received like an announcement of what everyone has been waiting for, like mail call at an army camp. Nearby unmated adults, not immediately engaged in the local activity, join in with even greater energy than the others. Such a tern might even open its bill and make a begging cry as if to say it was only a week old itself and needed a handout. They are always ready to scream out, to chase and be chased at all times, but even the *threat* of robbing seems to result in a show of latent excitement that pulses up and down on command.

The center of all this intense activity is itself on fire with spontaneity. A tern chick scarcely hatched, looking wobbly, incapable, and infirm, can literally bounce off the ground with excitement when a parent offers it a fish. Older chicks waiting to be fed hop up and down and jump around, begging and screeching like noisy toys on springs. A chick that strays away from the space where it is defended by its parents, and goes too near other birds brooding and feeding their young, is often pecked for the transgression. When attacked, chicks crouch down submissively, but this may not be enough to make an adult cease and desist. The young can be savagely pecked, if seldom killed. Death by exposure is more common. A few days of cold, wet, and stormy weather can be lethal to the very young, with their undeveloped feathers. This is particularly true of Arctic terns nesting in the more northerly regions of the Atlantic coast.

One summer in Maine, my son Charlie and I had taken out the skiff and traveled between the islands to reach a rocky islet where perhaps a hundred pair of common terns had nested the year before. We landed there—while the birds flew up and hovered overhead— made a quick count of the nests, and left. For whatever reason, relatively few chicks scuttled for cover into the scanty vegetation, the rocky nooks and crannies. Many lay dead, some eggs were rotten, others contained dead chicks that had been about to hatch. Had the colony deserted because of predation, or severe disturbance? I found it hard to guess, but it appeared that the adults which were still there were not attending to chicks or eggs with much intensity.

(On another islet, twenty minutes to half an hour beyond this one, forty to fifty terns had nested the year before. Johnny Thompson, who ran a lobster pound nearby, told us that some boys had come out from town in a boat and shot a number of birds, so that the rest of them deserted.)

Small colonies in the first place, less well protected by force of numbers and aggressive defenders, are less vigorous. When these are doing badly, chicks are fed less often and in smaller quantities, with the predictable result that their growth is poor and they often starve to death. These weak and neglected chicks are easily killed by predators, and their parents do not do much to protect them. Even at the beginning of the season, colonies conspicuously lacking in vigor lay smaller clutches with often smaller eggs than normal, incubate them less faithfully, and feed their chicks less well after they are hatched.

Having often delighted in those noisy, jumping, bombastic chicks farther to the south, I found the evidence on that Maine island very sad. A dead chick, lying on the sand, or on rocky ground in its nest of scanty humus, grass, or rockweed, is nothing but a pinch of down, a flattened bit of dried fluff with a beak and two legs. Where has all that fierce insistence gone that spoke for the race of terns all over the globe? Immortal eagerness seemed pathetically served.

Yet I was looking in on them from the outside, as if I did not belong with these birds, they who are so much a part of Mortality. That this vital charm and energy could be so quickly crushed can give anyone feelings of pity, which are not compensated for by thinking that, after all, these little ones are as expendable as tadpoles, pollen grains, or the progeny of marine fish. Still it is life's passage through death that created them. Without death, this leaping into the light would not be possible. Nothing has left the newly born behind. They have come out of the immortal wilderness, fitted to meet storms and fire on the sea, and darkness by land. They were never designed for finality. It was man, as the poet Yeats put it, who created death.

Fishing

1

The surf booms in the distance, where the waves meet a long line of outer bars; it is a sound without words, an expression from the beginning. Sea music joins the wind, while the light of the sun, giver of life, breaks through the clouds and spangles the water. In the words of an ancient Brahman prayer, spoken at dawn, "May the sun quicken our minds."

The terns are a measure of light in their intense responses, with the dark rules of night lying in their small heads. I am always conscious of the pull of distance in them, as the waves, out of their long sea hauls, lope through eternities. They have affinities with water, long lasting, ever present. Stretched out when posturing, with glistening plumage, a soft gray that reflects the clouds, they remind me of fish. Suddenly, a big flock rises off the shore in a cascade of sound. They circle, rise, and fall over the water, screaming out as one voice, a centralization of force, entreating the elements.

Nothing seems to go entirely easy with these savage beauties. It is hard to guess what their agitated behavior means at any given moment, as if we were only half aware of what they are responding to. It is we who are so often in the dark. All the rational explanations we can bring to bear on their behavior never quite catch up with the rhythmic performance of the whole community, in its interchanges with a world we have not yet discovered.

In June, while they are incubating eggs and, after the middle of the month, brooding chicks, there is no let-up in the feeling of urgency in the colony. In fact, it increases. The birds are almost constantly on the alert. Individuals head out on fishing expeditions, flying long and low across the surface of the water, often dipping their bills into it, if they have delivered food to their young, and then are lost to sight. When they return with fish, they are furiously chased. Any fish carrier, even when landing at its own nest, arouses some excitement in the neighbors. In a large colony, an increase in aggressive chasing may be the result of a sparsity of food. In some areas, they occasionally take to robbing each other, just as laughing gulls occupying the same territory as the terns may mob one as it comes in with a fish. They harry it, like parasitic jaegers, which chase both gulls and terns to make them drop their food.

A tern shows every kind of ability to elude its pursuers, twisting and dodging, swooping down, swinging aside, and lifting up again. Its long, narrow wings lack the speed of a shorebird's. They are built for hovering, but they are also highly maneuverable. They can beat their way into the wind, plying it with an easy, rowing motion, and then shift all of a sudden to the side, to fling back downwind with an abandon that suggests they enjoy it.

Robbing is not all uniform. It may be entirely absent in some colonies, occur randomly in others, or suddenly become a widespread local habit. So far as I have been able to find out, robbing between adults occurs when a colony is under exceptional stress. Some years ago, the terns at Plymouth, Massachusetts, had been suffering from a reduced supply of fish in adjacent waters, and they took to piracy, as the ornithologists have called it. A certain number of parents even got most of the food for their chicks this way.

≈

Stray individuals may take to piracy too, and are very skillful in their trade. On the coast of Norfolk, England, I saw a roseate tern flying rapidly back and forth over a patch of sandy ground where there were a few nests. Then it began to dip up and down, and suddenly, quicker than my eye could follow, it snatched a fish from the bill of a common tern that was carrying it down to the nest. The victim never had a chance to duck, but stopped in midflight, looking stunned by the disappearance of its fish.

Life in a ternery is one not only of rhythmic exchanges that are a pleasure to watch, but of common greed; the taking of unfair advantage, plus an unavoidable tendency to petulance, are fundamental too. Not that this fails to add a certain familiar reality to the whole performance. None of us is so elevated as not to recognize the pirate within; it often enslaves us.

If terns have trouble finding fish, they may switch to an alternate food, such as salt marsh killifish, or shrimp. Because of their wildly fluctuating environment, the source of supply will shift its locations naturally, from year to year. It may also be affected by human development, on its present, all-pervasive scale, if to a varying, unpredictable extent. Now, or in the long run, polluted and overfished waters make barren providers.

I once visited an island in Bull Bay, South Carolina, where royal and sandwich terns were nesting, as well as brown pelicans. The royal, second only to the Caspian in size, is a warm water bird whose range on both sides of the American continent is restricted to warmer currents. When these currents shift, the royal may extend or limit its range accordingly, as it follows species of warm water fish, up to some four inches long. These include young herring, bluefish, and squid, plus silversides and menhaden. They have also been known to snatch fish from the pouches of their neighbors, the brown pelicans. Royals nest in small numbers in Europe, and on sandy beaches along the northwest coast of Africa.

Black skimmers, tern relatives that nest all the way from Cape Cod south to Florida, are also found along these shores. They nest in many small colonies, feeding in shallow water in the tide pools and channels that thread the marshes. On this same trip, I had watched a group of them on the Gulf coast, as they rose with a wheeling surge into the air, then dipped and cruised low over the surface of the water on long, sinuous wings. They plowed it lightly as they went, with their curiously shaped long bills that snap shut like a pair of scissors on the fish they stir up. Because this is a tactile response, rather than one of sight, Skimmers are able to feed at dusk or during the night, and so avoid competition with fishing terns. There was a wonderfully supple beat to those thin-edged wings. As they stood in the shallows, I noticed that some dipped up water to use it when preening their feathers. Since it was springtime, one pair exchanged a few ceremonious bows and then stood apart in great composure. They faced into a light wind, holding their proboscis-like bills in front of them. I could hear a slight "uhk-uhk," as if they were quietly musing and humming to themselves. When disturbed, they flew off with a cry of "ahnk-ahnk," like horns at a New Year's party.

Out beyond the channeled marshes where an oystercatcher wheeled by like a discus, and snowy egrets lifted up, classically white, the small island lay out in the shallow waters of Bull Bay, behind a long barrier beach. The refuge manager took me out in his boat and we landed on a narrow strip of sand which encircled hummocks and higher ground where the pelicans nested. At the center of the island was a marshy area with nesting willets.

Each pair of pelicans had an area of about four square feet of nesting space. This bird is one of nature's exotics, grotesque but well finished, with multicolored feathers and an odd, downward-hanging, pouched beak. It was made to look grave and strange, doubtless for grave and strange reasons. The white, chocolate, cream, and yellow color of their heads and necks, the grizzled brown on their backs and wings, contrasted vividly with the beach and mist colors of the trim-bodied terns. When we got to within twelve to fifteen feet of them, where they sat ponderously on their bulky nests, they raised their heavy wings and silently took off, with quick, sure strokes. Anyone who has seen them effortlessly gliding along the surfline knows how synchronized they are with the rhythm of the waves. They are masterful flyers, soaring up to great heights in the sky.

The royal terns were ranked along the beach, a handsome company with distinctive black crests and orange bills. They had a ready, nervous, upward-looking way of carrying themselves, like thoroughbred horses. "Brrahk!" they cried, as they took off elegantly into the air. Their wings had a longer, looser motion than that of the smaller Sandwich terns farther down the beach. These two species often associate.

Because it was early in the season, the royals were not yet nesting, but I could see a few engaging in aerial courtship high overhead, and they had already made some bare scrapes in the sand. Later on, their eggs would be scattered along the beach like so many white stones. Both the Sandwich and the royals nested closely and noisily nearby, though in separate, compact groups. The waters around the island were only two or three feet deep and the tides were negligible. That meant that the nests close to the high-tide line were normally safe, but spring storms sometimes washed them out, and the birds would have to start all over again. In this region, royals laid only one egg, very rarely two, which does not necessarily indicate, as I heard it suggested later on, that this was a protective adaptation in the face of losses by spring storms. Other species lay small clutches, and the evidence shows that this relates to the shifting nature of the food supply, often scarce, and the competition for it. Also, royals feed their young for an unusually long period after they are fledged, up to seven months in fact, while they are developing the skillful fishing techniques they will need in order to survive. Since this is exacting for the parents, there would seem to be a definite advantage in their not having too many chicks to take care of.

To share these watery territories requires special abilities. Each species of tern has its own manner of getting food. The royals travel long distances from their colonies, searching for schools of fish, often driven to the surface by bluefish. The commons, feeding on smaller prey, like silversides and sand launces, may also travel some distance away from land, but they depend to a great extent on the shallow, inshore waters not too far from their nesting sites. The roseates, with more streamlined, less chunky bodies than the commons, and with shorter wings, can plunge as much as a foot deeper into the water and so reach fishes not easily available to the other. They can fly perhaps 50 percent faster, and will travel out to dependable fishing grounds.

The heavier Sandwich terns may fly even farther out than the roseates for their food, thirty to forty miles offshore. When diving in, they almost totally immerse themselves, staying under for several seconds, and so reach the fish that frequent different levels from those reached by the smaller commons and roseates.

The sooty and noddy terns of tropical waters are not plunge divers but snatch small fish and the larvae of flying fish out of the air as they skip over the surface, attacked by predatory fish beneath it. Brown noddies and sooties breed in the Dry Tortugas off Florida, while the latter also nests on islands off the coasts of Texas and Louisiana. The brown noddy and the black noddy have overlapping ranges which extend over vast areas of tropical seas, from the Atlantic to the Pacific. They feed within fifty miles of where they nest. The sooty, on the other hand, travels hundreds of miles from its territories, spending most of its life on the wing. As described in *The Oceanic Birds of South America*, it is "one of the most abundant sea birds throughout the pan-tropical oceans, nesting in the sands of countless islands in numbers that beggar description." Robert Cushman Murphy, the author of that landmark book, was a cultivated gentleman who was an admirer of Dante's *Divine Comedy*. When a young man, he voyaged on one of the last of the old time whaling vessels, the *Brig Daisy*. And as a traveler over the southern seas himself for many fruitful years, he wrote of the sooties, that after gorging themselves on fish, "they spend much time in aerial maneuvers, and sometimes joining the frigate birds in soaring higher and higher until they are lost to sight."

There is probably no more dramatic sight in the world than the eruption of the surface of the seas by countless numbers of prey fish.

One summer day, I traveled out with a boatload of people to look for whales, over a sea of golden-cloudy surfaces. It was a day of revelations, of unexpected magic in a recognizable world. That stretching mirror carried flying litter from off the land. Silky seeds sailed by on light, offshore winds, and even some fluttering butterflies. A dragonfly skimmed by the boat. Then seabirds materialized out of the distance, racing back and forth over the surface. They were working over an area where the ocean looked as if it had split its sides. There was a seething white band, or windrow, across it, where leaping, flipping fishes were escaping their pursuers, for half a mile or so. I had never seen such a passionate expression of earth's hunger before; it rose from the blood of the sea, whose moon-tide lives shared in its timeless depths.

A few miles farther out, and a finback whale was spotted. First we saw the waterspout, like a head of steam or a geyser, which was followed by the breaching of an enormous back, like a rock emerging from jostling tidal waters. After that, the dark shining body, some sixty feet long, arched forward and down in sinuous mobility, a great diving wheel with a curved fin raking behind it. The turbulent sea skin closed over it as it roamed below us through running schools of fish.

We almost lose these ancient circumstances in our self-enclosed wilderness. It is only through these adherents of enduring life, in their profound association, that we can rejoin the process, to follow eternal moments where fish and seabirds fly. I think I had never felt so close to the world sea and my own land as on that day.

2

The matter of depth at which various fish and crustaceans occur is of critical importance to the terns, especially where an accustomed food supply gives out. On the year when the supply of fish began to fail for the colony at Plymouth, Massachusetts, the common terns changed over to shrimp, which subsequently made up about two thirds of their diet. They were mainly a species of mud shrimp which the birds could only reach during the two or three hours of the ebbing tide. As a result, food was scarce, many chicks died of star-vation, and some of the parents, as I have said, took to piracy.

From the rejected fish lying on the ground, you can get a rough, if incomplete, idea of what the terns are catching offshore. On one islet in Maine, I found sea herring, alewives, cunners, and stickle-backs, even a little spiny-bodied sea robin. On the Cape, when there was an abundance of silversides and sand launces, this was primarily what I saw, plus young alewives. On Great Gull Island, there were pipefish, anchovies, mackerel, and butterfish, among others. Terns along the more southerly reaches of the coastline might catch silver-sides, mullet, pollock, and flounder. The royals, congregating over schools of fish at a long distance from their islands, were found to have brought in twenty species to their young along the eastern shore of Virginia and Delaware Bay.

So the kinds of fish to be found vary with the locality, and they vary as well in abundance and in the times they appear, from day to day and from week to week. Some years show a far greater variety than others. Occasionally, one species of fish leaves a region alto-gether. The fry of hake were once abundant in the shallow waters off Nantucket Island, and provided a major part of the diet for terns breeding and fishing in that area. When they disappeared, the birds were obliged to switch to other food.

(Terns have always been opportunistic enough to adjust to fluc-tuations in the food supply. Development, on the other hand, pressed on by a greatly increasing population on both coasts of America, reckless about the future, now threatens to bury earth's selective skills, wiping out, or thinning down, vital species before they have a chance to regenerate. Marine organisms are being contaminated by sewage outfalls, oil spills, chemical wastes, pesticides, and plastic. Inshore environments, such as marshes, streams, and estuaries where fish are nurtured, have been covered over, filled in, and eradicated on a major scale. It is as if the restorative links between land and sea are being cut, while the abundant trade of fishing peoples, men or terns, is left behind to take its chances on a diet of vacant waters.)

Larger colonial birds, such as gulls and cormorants, spend far less time and effort than the terns in getting food. They store food in their crops and feed their chicks by regurgitation, not having to fly many miles to catch a single fish. Each parent supplies enough to feed the entire brood when it returns from a fishing trip, with the result that a pair can alternate, sharing the brooding and fishing equally. Parent terns, on the other hand, may both be absent after the chicks are a few days old and have left the nest. They are often intensely busy from dawn to dusk, flying out and returning, feeding the young until they are three or four weeks old. In one area it was estimated that, on the average, common terns were returning to the nest with food every 16.6 minutes, though feeding rates can vary a great deal, depending on the food supply and the growth of the young.

The roseate feeds on schools of small marine fish, primarily sand launces in the northeastern part of their range, and it can dive in for them deeply and from greater heights than the common is capable of. Common terns, feeding on a greater variety of fish, in inshore as well as offshore waters, will occasionally hawk after flying insects. But now and then flocks of both species join together when small fish are driven to the surface by bluefish or striped bass.

At the outfall of a power plant on the Cape Cod Canal, the surface water is from twenty to twenty-five degrees warmer than the water four feet beneath it. In this area of turbulence, where warm water meets with cold, small fish are momentarily shocked, turn belly up, and are swept to the surface before they can right themselves. There they are tossed around like so many shiny slivers, easy prey for gulls as well as terns.

As I have walked out over the sandy flats, swum off the beaches, or sailed offshore, I have watched the terns traveling by and fishing all summer long. They fly over the water and when they spot fish, they hover, heel over, plummet in, then bob up to fly off again, with or without one in their bills. When hovering, preparatory to diving, they dexterously fan their wings, while pliantly spreading and drawing in their tails. They are intensely preoccupied. One summer day, I watched a single tern from a rowboat on a Maine cove. It was winging toward me from side to side, low over the water, so concentrated on scanning the surface that it hardly seemed to notice my boat, veering away just as it reached me.

Whether or not terns can catch fish, not tomorrow but now, can make the difference between life and death. A vessel can stay out for a week, moving from one fishing ground to another far offshore. This is a margin that terns, who have to return to their nests, can ill afford. In fact, the birds that are most successful are the ones that can switch from one kind of fish to another within their range, not losing precious time in hunting for what has grown scarce.

To succeed, the hunter's senses must be very keen. The arrow must hit the target, though it may often fall short. Terns seem tireless, trying again and again before they come up with a fish in their bills. Now and then, one appears on the territory carrying several fish at a time. Perhaps it found a heavy concentration and was inspired to keep picking them up, but it is not clear just how this is done. Some may become specialists in the art.

On Great Gull Island, a common tern brought in nine small fish at once to its chicks. They spared no time as the fish splattered over the rocks before them, rushing around in a frenzy, picking them up and gobbling them down.

After hovering over fish swimming just below the surface, a tern dives blind. Their sight is virtually useless underwater, unlike birds such as sea ducks, auks, loons, or pelicans; but over water, those big, black eyes, bulging a little on either side of their heads and occupying a large part of their heads, have superb sight. Like other seabirds, their eyes are equipped with an area of precise vision called the linear fovea, giving them a point of reference in relation to the marine horizon. Terns also have color vision, which may be complex enough to make their view of the world very different from our own.

A small flock hovers over shallow waters running out from a tidal creek across the brown sands of the flats at low tide. They keep dipping in with easy, shallow dives. What are they finding? I walk toward them, scaring them off, and at first I can see nothing in the water. Then flashing bursts of silver materialize, where tiny, almost transparent fish flicker over the bottom. The glaring sunlight makes wavy patterns across the fast-moving current, and it surprises me that the terns were able to catch anything at all. The reflection of light on the water is extremely misleading and a fish may be well below where you think you see it. Water in motion on an outgoing tide, under light wind and sun, is nothing I can catch.

Hovering when the wind is light and the surface fairly calm means that the terns have to remain stationary, and this requires more effort. Also fish can see the tern vigorously flapping its wings overhead and more easily avoid it. Against a moderate wind, on the other hand, terns hover with less effort, and the fish are less able to see them under a ruffled surface. Heavier winds and rougher seas where fish swim at deeper levels make a fishing tern's work much harder.

After I walk away for a short distance, some of the birds fly back, to hover over the current again. Their wings beat rapidly. Then, as they spot the fish ahead of them, they pitch forward, twisting a little as they dive in, wings closed, or partly closed, depending on the depth at which the fish are swimming. This untiring practice in the dynamic employment of the shallow seas is what the race depends on.

Vision, in its less material sense, is in the mind's eye, seen in a dream, or in a trance. The original native people of America followed the wilderness from which all fundamental dreams must come, and found "spirit helpers" who would guide them for the rest of their lives. Through "vision quests" individuals worshipped the eagle—the supernatural buffalo—or the morning star. A Plains Indian told anthropologist Robert Lowie that he had a feather which he kept as a remembrance of his vision of a bird, and that it was the greatest treasure in the world. Behind the tangible lies the revelation of the spirit.

One might argue that vision in our violent, contemporary world embraces disconnected dreams and public hallucinations, since we have been disengaged from an intangible entity we call the environment. The animals, on the other hand, not knowing any alternative, as we might put it, but simply knowing, keep the earth in being.

Out of endless periods of trial and error, the terns know their direction and location, through exceptional abilities of sight and inner timing, moving as the earth moves. We do not apply vision in this sense to a bird. We assume that sight is a mechanical feature that describes adaptation and closeness to habitat, but below that spirit cannot be called upon in any useful way. This implies that it is we who do not know, and may have lost our way. As the terns are true fishermen, we can at least call on them to tell us where the food of the spirit can be found.

Animals, to our way of thinking, do not behave religiously, though we can hardly refuse them their role in ceremony. Surely the ritualistic behavior of the terns obeys the outward signs of an inner grace, which cannot be monopolized by the human race. Why should fish, so central to their existence, not be sacred to the terns? At the very least, they are actors on behalf of what can never be transgressed.

In the morning, the braided sands lead off at low tide under a light fog, through which the sunlight has started to burn. The south wind cuffs away at sheets of shallow water, making feather patterns of purple and gray. A pair of roseates are out on the tidal flats, acting out the primal style. Seen from behind, the female, head and neck proudly stretched, has her wings parted like a bow that reminds me of the shape of a horseshoe crab, or of a flounder. The male, partly bent, holds a fish, a glint of silver in the drifting fog.

A fish, of the great race of fishes, with the color of reflecting waters. They are a sunset-yellow; coppery; pink and red; a steely blue; intensely silver like a herring, or a smelt; blue-black, green, and tawny yellow like a mackerel. There is no end to the changing reflections of light and water, as witnessed in their scales. In courtship, a fish becomes more than a food; it is a symbol, the ritualized body of the world.

It is a strange thing, when you first become aware of it, to see in these birds the transmutation of substance into the realm of the spirit, but "stereotyped ritual" is hardly enough. One day, watching this performance, I thought to myself: "Why, of course! 'This is my body.'"

Food has always been central to religious rites. And the human ceremonials that join a family through food and wine, or wife to husband, are not alien to a tern's offering of a fish to its prospective mate.

The fish, so profoundly a part of the tern's life and livelihood, and with which it must feel some irreplaceable attachment, is also a mark of what must live forever. As a ceremonial object, it indicates that what it symbolizes cannot be utterly consumed. In all this basic ritualizing might be the seeds of the human concept of immortality.

The fish itself is a mystery, as well as a known reality. The first spring alewives migrating into freshwater, flashing through the rocks of a down-falling stream, are silver spearheads thrown in by the energy of an unknown sea. I who am also of the living store of earth meet them symbolically. I now see fish in the way I first did, before a later age when I might imagine that experience had taught me better. So the terns themselves seem all youth and no old age.

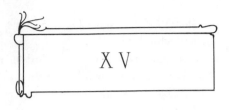

Growing Up

Spring into summer, the shorter days move on, while the tidal sea lunges against the shore, back and forth, in and out, with the regularity of breath. We complain about what we are doing to the planet and to each other, watching the news on television, counting the days. "Time flies." The terns, on the other hand, are timed to the revolutions of the wind.

Egg laying is timed according to the length of day and the warmer temperatures of early spring. Foraging for food is often highly dependent on the daily 12.4-hour cycle of the tides. As with other animal species, reproduction in terns may be influenced by the phases of the moon. It has been discovered that the breeding cycles of the tropical sooty terns on Ascension Island approximate the ten lunar cycles. The young in a temperate zone grow up at a time when food is most abundant, and migrate when it begins to be scarce. So time has meaning in terms of a seabird's inner responses to a rhythmically responsive planet. Clouds change shape and nature as summers pass. Those tern chicks that survive incessant mortality grow with astonishing speed, to follow the light away. We, who only follow money and the clock, are left behind.

In any given season, nesting should be finished for the majority by June 15, and some of the young will have fledged by July 10. By mid-August, activity is about over, and the terns that have not already left will start to flock away. Since the call of the community is stronger in them late in the summer than the need for individuals to go on rearing their young, chicks not fledged by this late date are deserted. This is a stark fact that needs to be thought of in context, within the great circle of the year.

The duration of light changes consistently, but it is hard to catch the time, as it disappears like the wake behind a ship. If there is an eternal moment, perhaps these seabirds catch it, diving like arrows to meet their needs, shifting in their motion with the changing atmosphere. On the nesting islands, out over the water, stroking buoyantly, hovering and dipping with limber ease, they follow unrelenting renewal. An outwardness grows in their feelings. They are called away. Soon they will leave this shore, though they will take its memory and location with them thousands of miles away.

Many of the young are already dividing their time between begging on the ground and making sporadic flights. Just how accomplished they are depends a good deal on their age. At three to four weeks they can fly short distances, and at about nine weeks they can fish for themselves, although some of the more precocious can do it earlier still. Even so, many young birds beg from their parents well into the fall. The juveniles of both commons and roseates are dependents for at least six weeks after fledging, and "can often be seen," according to Dr. Ian Nisbet, "in close company with one or two adults, even in places far from the breeding colony. Juveniles probably migrate south with their parents and may remain dependent on them for part of the first winter."*

The little ones keep flapping their wings as they develop. At first,

---

*Ian C. T. Nisbet, "The Roseate Tern," Reprint from the *1989/1990 Audubon Wildlife Report*, National Audubon Society.

they just shake their stumps, but with the growth of feathers and wing muscles, they will also jump and dance as they fan the air. It is a joy to see a nearly fledged chick eagerly facing its breast toward the sea, and beating its wings in such a hearty way, on the very brink of achievement. They *ask* you to cheer them on. First flights occasionally end with a tumble on the ground, or a crash landing over the water, so that they have to swim back. But they keep at it indefatigably, day after day. At first they only fly a few yards, then farther and farther, until they finally take off and land again with a hint of skill.

While they are hopping and spreading their wings against the wind, they also show signs, even on the ground, of feeding for themselves. Now and then a newly feathered chick will pick up a bit of thatch or seaweed and toy with it, or make a futile scurry in the direction of a moth as it flies by.

Watching these minor acts, I have felt elated to think how ordinary discovery has to be to satisfy me. Once I sighted an adult common tern eating a brown and orange butterfly. The insect's wings fell off as the bird ate its body, and I felt as I had made a great find for the day.

Their first spontaneous flights over the water seem unexpected, perhaps because they are arrived at so gradually. Unless you can spend your entire time watching a single bird, its stages of transition can only be guessed at. Then, one day the practice seems to start all over the colony, with juveniles making brief swoops offshore, picking up bits of debris and dropping them again.

As more of them reach the flying stage, they are more randomly distributed over the ternery, some bunched together, others at various distances from their original nesting areas. They find hiding places where they wait to run out when a parent flies in with food. On the verge of flight, many start moving closer to the edge of the colony. Some walk in to the water to bathe.

There is a natural teasing involved in getting a chick to feed for itself. An adult will fly down and stand next to a six- or seven-week-old chick that is screeching for food, but without a fish; and the young one pokes in a futile way at the parent's bill. Once I watched a young bird that waited for its parents for an hour and a half, and when one of them finally showed up with no fish and started to leave again, it pattered off too as if needing to fly. Occasionally a fledgling will fly up briefly after an adult stranger as it cruises by with a fish in its bill.

A fish too big for a nearly grown chick to manage is brought in by a parent and left lying on the ground. At first the parent pokes at the fish as if to encourage its offspring to take it, but the chick seems uninterested. So the adult takes the fish in its bill and flies out over the water. The chick lifts up off the ground and follows, only to see the parent drop the food into the water in an unconcerned manner, losing it for both of them. The young bird then makes a few shallow swoops toward the surface as if it meant to try fishing on its own, a trial practice in the art.

This continued exercise in flight and fishing is encouraged by the fact that a seven-week-old chick no longer scurries for cover when alarmed, but lifts into the air. So when an adult takes an idly aggressive peck at it, it can fly off. At this stage, well on in the summer, individual adults begin to be less intense about foraging for food, and the demands of their young are not so often met. Withholding fish also has the effect of making the juveniles less bound to the ground. Then, chasing after their parents in the air strengthens their flying skills.

Although the adults lead the young out to fly, they do not actually teach them to fish. It seems that the art of fishing is as much provoked as it is learned by example. The young are partly agitated into practicing their innate skills and, of course, consistent hunger, combined with the inner need to move away, must play its role.

To see them achieve the moment of flight is to realize that the practice of growth is unfailing, in all of life. Young terns are called ahead; in them is the magnet of distance.

There are always a certain number of unmated birds that linger in the area after the rest have left. The high flights of courtship can still be seen. Fish are being carried in flight or offered and withheld on the ground, rituals that will not be completed except as another year allows it. Unfledged chicks, whose future does not look promising, are still engaging in tugs of war over fish, and this sometimes occurs between roseate and common terns that are being fed in the same vicinity. The young are always highly enthusiastic about running out and snatching what they can get, whether it is meant for them or not. Usually a parent hesitates before landing to feed its own young if there are too many others in the same area. Running interference from other adults to begin with, as they swoop down toward the ground, they are liable to be mobbed by all the hungry chicks in the vicinity. If the fish is not instantaneously grabbed and swallowed, someone else not in the family will pick it off the ground, or even try to take it away from a young bird with a fish head disappearing down its gullet.

Certain patterns repeat themselves in the life of terns, as they do in our own lives. The behavior of a female tern during courtship displays reminds you of a chick ardently begging for food. Its rapidly repeated "ki-ki-ki-ki-ki" is much the same sound, though harsher, less musical, that she makes with lowered head while a male is pattering around before her with a fish in his bill. She begs, half resistant, half tempted to grab the fish. He offers and at the same time withholds. both are constrained. Ritualization serves a profound purpose in the life of terns on a breeding colony and, I would suppose, after they leave it, if in a less concentrated way. When such ambivalent impulses are resolved in courtship displays, high flights, or changeovers at the nest, it amounts to an emancipation. We too reach mutual formalities out of those realms of light which rule us through no will of our own.

Begging in the young gets louder and more persistent as they grow. They often sound determined enough to be calling anything within earshot, or even the sky itself. A juvenile not fully feathered out will even beg from a recently fledged bird as it flies over. More hunger makes them more aggressive. When food is short, growing chicks will attack others with even greater passion than they normally show when they see them being fed.

≈

I see in them an elemental desire, an inner, irresistible impatience implying a later capacity to seize the moment. In their begging, I see that all life must fly like the light for its fulfillment, against the will of time, the fact of attrition. We know this in ourselves. Certainly those small birds do not have the great dichotomies of humor, or its lack, of hate and love, joy and despair, that we experience. Yet their inner world, stripped of that human capacity, responds to earth's profundity. In their behavior, they too are reconcilers of opposites. A perpetual fusion sustains life on the planet. Conscious control does not bypass original attachment. The rituals we both act out were not invented by one race and unconscious in the other.

To beg is everything. An often tragic wanting is the most binding sense we have. I beg, therefore I am, the weight of earth, and even that escape from earth which makes man envious of space, inside me.

On that centrifugal territory, to which the terns are drawn and which they are soon to leave, chicks are still hopping and screeching. Adult pairs still posture, with gestures half defiant, half appeasing. They go on begging, fishing, feeding their young, but there is a restlessness in them that moves with the season. They begin to gather together more, bathing and fishing in small flocks along the shore. There are markedly fewer birds on the colony. Many have already left, either because their young are fledged, or because their nesting has failed. Juveniles, with white foreheads instead of the all black heads of the adults, are among the first to leave. Their parents often go with them, following them as they fly off, or the young will follow the parents.

At this stage, the plumage of the young has a tawny look, with bits of down wisping up between their feathers. They still beg with chattering, machine-gun rapidity, but they are beginning to be more adept. They have not yet learned the complexities of plunge diving, but they hover and swoop across the surface. They have short tails and their wings are not fully developed. At first they only pick things awkwardly off the water, such as the floating swim bladder of a sea-weed. They lack poise and have to work hard against even a moderate wind. They seem to tire easily and settle back on the ground, but they keep growing in skill.

After dispersing from their respective territories, small flocks are now fishing, resting, and feeding their young along the shore. I see them flying past like clouds before the wind.

Those still lingering on their nesting sites in late summer may move off at varying times on impulse. One outflight was described to me as it occurred at Great Gull Island. At dusk, a group of several hundred suddenly flew off from the edge of the island in complete silence, almost as one organism. Like a turning school of fish, they swooped low over the water. As they rose up from it, they all started calling out at once, in apparent confusion. Then they headed back to the shore, where they spread out, to spontaneously fly out again later on.

J. M. Cullen has written of evening flights made by Arctic terns in which as many as forty or fifty would ascend into the air until they reached an altitude of several hundred feet.* Then they would begin to fly off on one course, only to shift to a second and even to a third, as if they had not yet decided on a particular direction. They moved with steady wing beats, disappearing, passing overhead, and then coming back into view, their feathers glinting against the sun. Were these flights another expression of unresolved feelings that only needed something to set them off?

Such flights seemed to have started with a panic, after which a few birds kept on rising high together and displaying, instead of returning to the ground. Then these few dropped out of the main flock and alighted, while the rest changed their pattern of flight, flying up, heads into the wind, their wings beating steadily. They were not bunched together, as in a panic, but flew loosely and a little apart, though closely oriented to one another at the same time. Some of these birds might return again to the ground, or continue on as migrants. They included both young and adults, and apparently such

---

*"A Study of the Behavior of Arctic Terns (*Sterna macrura*)," Thesis deposited at Bodleian Library, Oxford, 1956.

flights only occurred in the evening. It has been suggested that there might be a correlation between the height at which the Arctics set off on migration and the time of day, another of those fascinating speculations that touch on the many formalities that make up the life of terns.

There is a quixotic quality about them that is hard for an observer to assess. It is like a wild dancing on the surface of the water which has no obvious cause. You can be fully aware of their responsiveness toward one another. You can feel the shifts in their motion as being appropriate to the moment. You can even define specific actions. But what really stimulates them is often undefinable. Perhaps this is only a way of naming the depths of the psyche. What is a tern? An impossible question. Either you say: "That is all they know, and what they are limited to," or you recognize some inescapable kinship in which earth directions are profoundly involved.

On the edge of departure into the wider world of the seas, the fringes of the continents, the terns begin to join the great migrations of the air. They do not all move out at once. Cape Cod becomes a center of passage, and a staging area, for commons and roseates nesting in northern areas on their way south, and even some that come from colonies to the south. They feed over shallow inshore waters, in August and September, on an abundance of small fish. And adults from local colonies are still feeding their young, out on sandbars at mid- to low tide, or on the banks of inlets.

After a hot afternoon in August that follows fog, rain, and a southwest wind the day before, the skies change again as it grows dark, with upward-sweeping clouds high overhead. As if to put on one final performance with which to crown the season, a pair of roseates fly so high in the air that I can hardly see them. They are swaying and swinging, passing over and under each other, slipping gradually across a saffron sun whose eye blinks through spreading clouds. It is an easy, loping interchange that lowers down like the light itself toward the sea.

XVI

Crossroads

On the coast of Maine, not far from the open waters of the Atlantic, lies a tiny island called Killick Stone, its rounded back lying low in the water. It is full of goldenrod, raspberry thickets, reeds, and grasses, with a center of thick turf riddled with holes made by mice. Seaside lavender, or marsh rosemary, grows along its stony shore, which has a small pocket of beach facing the mainland, composed mostly of shell fragments. A perky song sparrow, mounted on a goldenrod, sings out with its high, sweet voice, piercing the waves of the enveloping sea air. A small number of terns have nested here. There is still a nest with two eggs in the middle of the island, and they are warm, though this is mid-August. There is no hope for them, but I am prompted to shorten my visit, in case a parent is present. There is also the body of a juvenile tern lying on the ground. Now liberated from the intensity of the breeding season, most terns along the coastline have moved away to the measure of fall winds and wider seas, leaving these aborted efforts behind them.

Just before I landed on the beach in my skiff, I saw a number of shorebirds there, a mixed flock of ruddy turnstones, black-bellied and semi-palmated plovers, which had touched down on their migration from the Arctic. While the whole sky seems to move out like the birds, there is a feeling of steadfast calm about this small island. Towering clouds rise out of the open ocean beyond it. A dolphin arches above the surface of the water. In the far distance, I can glimpse the disappearing body of a small whale as it makes its dive. Many lobster boats are running by. The lobstermen stop by their buoys and pull up their traps, check them, and throw them and rejected lobsters back into the water, almost with one motion. Then they gun the motor and the boat drones on. The order of the year pulls men and birds with it, while schools of small fish run by the shore, sweeping past in the clear water, hesitating, turning back. A loon rides offshore like a carved boat. And a great flotilla of young eider ducks, accompanied by female adults, has gathered off a larger island a few hundred yards away. There the tidewaters lunge in and swash back and forth against its rocky sides, lifting and releasing the skirts of golden rockweed. Here is the center of the circumnavigations of the globe. I would be nowhere else on earth.

There are many such crossroads and gathering places where birds and fish meet and separate, feed and move on. A major one is in the shallow waters between Monomoy Island and the mainland shores of the Cape. Their depth is some twelve feet, twenty where the bottom shelves off into Nantucket Sound. Terns feed here during migration over shoal waters where bumps and hollows on the bottom shelter bait fish that are periodically heaved up to the surface by tidal currents, or chased up by bluefish. The rhythmic feeding of the terns coincides, in other words, with the presence of fish in constantly changing currents, and it is often dramatic to watch. At the end of September of 1988, when the tag-end effects of hurricane Hugo were being felt along the eastern shore, big rollers were smashing in over the long barrier beach to the north end of these waters. At high tide, this had the effect of stirring up large numbers of small fish, and many terns were diving in to catch them. As the tide lowered, they began to move in over the shallow water and fish there.

At this time, an estimated 10,000 tree swallows on their southerly migration were hawking for insects over the marshy center of Monomoy Island. They were flying fast and low in all directions over the ground.

The first wave of terns, 80 percent of them roseates and 20 percent commons, perhaps 3,000 in all, arrive at this staging area in early August. Many of the roseates come here after nesting on Bird Island in Marion, Massachusetts, not far away, the majority being fledglings. Ed Moses and David Houghton of the U.S. Fish and Wildlife Refuge took me out in their boat toward nightfall on the 9th of August. Hundreds of terns were resting on sandbars, their bodies a twinkling white as the light began to fade. Many others were hurrying over the surface, scattered far and wide. Young roseates, looking chunky without the conspicuous tails of the adults, and a gleaming white underneath like a fish, were flying past us. Occasionally, there were adults and young flying together.

To the west, the glowing fireball of the sun was setting behind a purplish, smoky haze; it began to flatten out as it sank, looking like an enormous Chinese lantern. Toward the south, the sky was a curving blue shell adorned with fiery clouds. These waters are a great open stage for converging life. Beyond them is the timeless, invading ocean, the supreme unifier of the planet.

The next wave of terns, a great many of them flying down from nesting islands in the Gulf of Saint Lawrence, is composed of commons. They begin to arrive by the thousands in late August and early September. When these migrants finally leave, by mid-October, they often go as family flocks, and follow the continental coastline south, as they do on their return migration in the spring. The roseates, superior flyers, head out to sea. Given enough calm weather, some may fly nonstop all the way to northern South America.

The terns of both species do not move off right away, in other words. Roseates from Great Gull Island in Long Island Sound have been sighted during September all the way north to Cape Cod, the Gulf of Maine, and Nova Scotia. Commons are locally seen during the autumn from Nova Scotia to the Carolinas. They range widely

≈

for weeks until, by November, most of them will have left the northeast coast for good. Roseates winter from the western coast of Colombia to eastern Brazil. The commons winter all the way from Florida down to Central America and Brazil. They are also sighted as far south as the Falkland Islands, off the southern tip of South America.

During the fall, I have watched fishing terns over Monomoy as they hit the water in such numbers that they sound like so many paddlewheels on a riverboat. They are continually pitching down out of their flocks and rising up again, with a continuous, furious motion like the waters of a fountain. Their wings beat tirelessly and steadily, with tails flexing and spreading apart. Occasionally, one will halt in mid-air, with a shuddering in its body. Beyond a fishing flock, which has found a large concentration of fish, individuals chase each other, making grating, excited cries, beating ahead in slipping, striding flight, lifting from side to side. Hundreds of shorebirds pipe and trill in the distance at low tide, and the "kleep-keeahlee" of black-bellied plovers, the "keearrh" of common terns, and the baying of black-back gulls accent their movements from one area to another.

Many juveniles are still fishing comparatively late in the season, making incomplete dives, dipping into the surface again and again. Miles from their original nesting sites, they roost along a beach, on offshore rocks or buoys, or even on the rim of a dory as it rocks on its mooring. They can be seen using the same roosts day after day. Some will fly up from time to time when a parent flies by. I have seen young commons fly after an adult, begging harshly, until it dives and comes up with a fish, which is presented to them in mid-air. With a couple of upward lunges, the young bird swallows the silver food in flight, like a man gulping down his food when he is in a hurry.

Through continual practice, and with the greater assurance that comes to them with experience, they practice plunge diving, beating upwind, and maneuvering back and forth, improving day by day. Where schools of fish fry are heavily concentrated, flashing at the surface of a cove or the mouth of a tidal creek, or far out over the flats where channel waters run by a sandbar, they can pick them up more easily. Watching this exercise, I can understand how fine a balance there is between skill and scarcity.

As the fall progresses, the young fly in a much more effortless way than when they were making short and awkward flights over the territory. Their wings have a sure beat, though they lack quite the pliant control they will acquire later on. Their cries are no longer the harsh, repetitive tones of a begging chick. By October or earlier the voice of a juvenile common changes from a dry, high-pitched, squeaky sound to something like the "keearrh" of an adult, a sort of trilling, short "keer."

During the first week in October, I have seen flocks of several hundred terns fishing at the mouth of an estuary, the kind of place where small fish also congregate heavily in the autumn. By this time, most of the adults have molted their summer plumage, so that they have white foreheads like the immature birds, and it becomes hard to tell one from the other at a distance. But the young are still gray and buff colored. They also have docked tails, and lack the red beak and legs of a breeding adult.

At the beginning of November, I have counted as many as forty or fifty terns at a time fishing over the tidal flats at low water. During the following days, I have seen a few along the shore, but no more large flocks on the horizon. One year, a few were seen slowly flying upwind during a Thanksgiving storm, and two or three terns were reported to have been seen in Provincetown Harbor as late as December.

Another autumn is moving on, and those harsh, expostulatory cries are nearly lost to my ears. Still, the ancient landscape of the tides is forever shifting before me, with its side-winding ripples between ribs of sand, its wandering pools and runnels streaked and lighted by sun and wind. The practiced reach—in need and in growth—that I have watched in this bird society since their arrival in May seems as relentlessly impelled as it is full of grace. The great exercise in the life of earth, of which they are such a beautiful example, makes terrible demands. At times I have thought that the nesting

~

season was like a protracted raid into enemy territory. What do they encounter but predators on all hands, killing weather, and, all too often these days, the destruction of their habitats? Yet they persist. There are profound implications in this about accommodation with nature and the earth. How could any of us, having faced a season of terns, afford to congratulate ourselves?

I watch from the shore to see the last terns of autumn easily drifting over deep water on the near edge of sandbars a mile or so away. They compensate in flight for the puffs and eddies of the wind. Their floating on is interrupted by liftings and fallings that parallel the rhythmic travel of the waves. As they race back at intervals and return, they reflect the sun, which turns them into brilliant shards and slivers of light.

Far out over the open water, now hard to see, even with my field glasses, a much larger flock seems to turn and hover in mid-air. Then it moves on as a cloud that streams out and gathers in again, a mass shifting in the sunlight, alternately showing white of breast and darker gray of wing. The flock swings off horizontally, spreading and gathering as it goes, disappearing into the hazy distance.

XVII

Inheritors of the Spirit

The first tern warden I ever met lived above a rattling, shingle beach on the west coast of England. He presided over a mixed colony of common and sandwich terns in sandy tidelands beyond the shore, and his father had been the warden before him. The town he lived in, with its modest, two-storied houses, had developed through centuries of accommodation to stormy seas. In fact, he introduced me to the terns as if they were a traditional part of his own community. He talked about them and their habits out of long experience, treating them as if they were his seasonal neighbors, not any more or less difficult than his year-round neighbors were likely to be.

In America, where accommodation with the land has seldom been achieved for long since the white man came, tern wardens are a relatively new breed. They are often college-trained people who take it on as a seasonal job, or they are volunteers who live in the neighborhood of a tern colony. They may also serve as employees of various agencies with a responsibility to try as best they can to protect the birds in terms of the emergencies that face them. The land and its native life have been treated for such a long time as a mere adjunct of the material needs of our society that it is almost becoming invisible. Habitat has no variety if you are unable to distinguish it from the asphalt; it becomes dematerialized.

A land stripped of its detail may sell a million house lots, but it has also lost its roots in the earth. The houses themselves have been deprived of a location. The sun rises without the trees, and the night has lost its company.

A society of machine owners has a tendency to think that it has a final right to everything it runs over, whether it is woodland, sand, or water. It would seem ridiculous to most people to imagine that a beach could be claimed through ancestral right by a beach flea or a bird, and that it would be barren without them. That is what comes of having just landed from the moon. We have hardly had enough time to explore the interior of the New World.

With another season passed and remembered, I think of those crowded summer beaches where no one is lonely but the terns. Hundreds, thousands of people are there, drinking beer, taking pictures of each other, happily playing volleyball, frying hamburgers, frying themselves in the sun, or lumbering through the sands in their campers or beach buggies. They co-exist, here and there, with a few, small, and scattered least tern colonies that shift their locations from year to year along Cape Cod's outer beach. Because of their soft, ash-gray feathers, they are hard to spot, and their presence often goes unnoticed.

When the need for roped-off areas where the terns nest is pointed out to people, and explained, they usually accept it. But what any warden encounters, and strives to overcome, is a certain mass indifference. We behave like a race apart. "Wildlife," the label we use for the animals, only describes the poverty of our feelings toward them.

One day, some years ago, I accompanied Dennis Minsky, now a schoolteacher, as he made his daily rounds as a tern warden for the Cape Cod National Seashore. He made a point of patiently talking to any individual or group coming too close to the nests. A big camper, with several occupants, almost drove through the ropes at one site.

≈

Dennis stopped them and they listened to what he had to say. He wore a park ranger's uniform. As they started to move off, I heard the man next to the driver murmuring, half in humor, "Don't drive over the tern warden, will you."

Those who monitor tern islands or patrol the beaches, night and day, are an admirable breed. They are not only dedicated to saving a species and its habitats, they encourage the rest of us to see, which implies a personal equation with what we see. To know the earth is to know its inhabitants, not just as names and numbers, but as extensions of ourselves. Otherwise, we live in a no man's land of our own making, warring indiscriminately on everything that seems irrelevant to us.

During many years of living by the waters of the Northeast, I have watched all kinds of landed elements disappear, from old dories to old speech, from independent farmers and fishermen to declining races of birds and fish. Thousands of local Indian sites are now buried under housing and commercial developments. Indian prayer that communicated directly with the spirit of the land lies buried with them. We now reach everywhere beyond those roots we had started to put down. Remoteness has almost been lost, and with that comes a loss of intimacy. Local sense and nurture has been replaced on a global scale because of our accelerated ability to reach everywhere through mechanical means, and to move out almost instantaneously from wherever we happen to be.

As we became independent of the places we lived in for our food, we grew in illusion. Starvation of the land led to exploitation of every unoccupied land beyond it. We became disengaged from our old home in the weather, and could no longer read its signs. Reports of it now arrive through automated machines. We are discovering, almost too late, that a nature dispossessed is no man's friend. What we desert starts lifeless deserts on the move.

At the same time, light reappears on the horizon for the eternal life and death reply to disengagement. Neither man nor tern can escape an unrelenting exposure to its truth. The terns are survivors of a game of high risk, played out through seas of elemental conflict and change. They live through milleniums in an hour. They follow a great continuum, like the waves forever curling and falling down the shores of the world. They are untiring, restless explorers of an earth which has always sustained them. Light-boned birds, lifting up excitedly as on a drawstring from the sun, they are committed to its sacred ancestry.

On a wall of the many Paleolithic caves in the Dordogne region of France, I recently saw the clear outline of a waterbird, perhaps a heron, an astonishing 20,000 years after it was etched in the rock. The eye of a bird, the minds of men, were brought together in the miraculous consistency of sight.

When my wife and I returned home from that trip, it was early in June, when the birds were still mating and building their nests. Two brilliantly colored Northern, or Baltimore, orioles, a male and a female, were chasing each other back and forth across a broad pattern of new leaves shining in the sun. they were calling out in beautiful flutelike tones, triumphantly proclaiming a bond that held the meaning of their year, of all the years. The triumph is not in us but in a perpetual timing.

In the last analysis, I do not know terns, any more than I know myself. They keep leading me toward any number of questions to which I only receive tangential answers. Still, they have enlarged my sight, my aspiration, my grasp of the earth's great distances. What more do we need to know than that the truth lies not in us alone, but with every other form of life, no matter how insignificant it may seem. How can Man, "Created from Everything," in the Navajo myth, live in a state of disengagement from Everything and still survive?

The world begins and ends in love, and unexplored affinities. A tiny hummingbird knows more than I do about the brilliance of its attachments. The future lies in a flower, and the mind of a bird.